THEORIES OF GENERAL EDUCATION

Theories of General Education

A Critical Approach

Craig C. Howard

St. Martin's Press   New York

First published in the United States of America in 1992

Printed in Hong Kong

ISBN 0–312–04743–6

Library of Congress Cataloging-in-Publication Data
Howard, Craig C.
Theories of general education : a critical approach / Craig C.
Howard.
p.   cm.
Includes bibliographical references.
ISBN 0–312–04743–6
1. General education.   2. Education—Philosophy.   I. Title.
LC980.H68   1992
370.11—dc20   90–30950
                                                          CIP

For the educators in my life:
especially my parents

Contents

Acknowledgements

Acknowledgement is made to copyright holders for permission to use the following copyrighted material: excerpts from *Democracy and Education* by John Dewey (New York: Macmillan, 1916); excerpts from *The Quest for Certainty: A Study of the Relation of Knowledge to Action* (New York: The Putnam Publishing Group, 1960); excerpts from *Legitimation Crisis* by Jurgen Habermas (Boston: Beacon Press, and Oxford: Basil Blackwell, UK, 1975); excerpts from *The Uses of the University*, 3rd edition, by Clark Kerr (Harvard: Harvard University Press, 1982); excerpts from *The Higher Learning in America* by Robert M. Hutchins (New Haven: Yale University Press, 1936).

Introduction

HISTORICAL BACKGROUND

The quality of undergraduate education in the United States has recently been called into question by a series of national reports. In October of 1984 the National Institute of Education issued a report citing a series of warning signals indicating that the quality of undergraduate education had declined (*The Chronicle of Higher Education*, 24 October 1984). In November of 1984, then chairman of the National Endowment for the Humanities, William J. Bennett, released an extensive report expressing concern for the lack of coherence and vitality in the undergraduate curriculum generally, and in the programs in the humanities in particular (*The Chronicle of Higher Education*, 28 November 1984). Finally, the Association of American Colleges released a report (*The Chronicle of Higher Education*, 13 February 1985) urging faculty to take responsibility for a return to quality teaching and curricular coherence in the face of increased emphasis on research, specialization, and fragmentation in the undergraduate curriculum.

All of these reports stressed the need for strengthening curricular coherence through some type of common general educational experience, and all of them lamented the specialized and vocational orientation of many undergraduate curricula. And while none of them made clear the normative ground from which they launched their critique of the status quo, all made recommendations for 'improving the quality' of education in the undergraduate colleges of America.

These concerns for quality in collegiate education are also articulated by writers and researchers of the nation's public schools. Ernest Boyer lists nine recommendations for improving the quality of education (1983: 7), and argues that our future as a nation depends on the quality of our nation's public education. John Goodlad (1984) also expresses concern for the quality of public school education and its articulation with the college experience. Mortimer Adler (1982), from a different point of view, would restructure public education so radically that its current practitioners would hardly recognize it. There is, has

1

been and will doubtless continue to be, increasing concern for
questions of quality at all levels of public education in the United
States.

These concerns are at least as old as the Yale Report of 1828
(Hofstadter and Smith, 1961: 275), perhaps the first American
apology for a classical and common curriculum to hold together
the moral fabric of the republic. Since the Yale Report, there
have been several periods of curricular reform in response to the
several vagaries of American history (Rudolph, 1977), and at
least three periods in the twentieth century when general
education was the special domain of curricular discussions
(Boyer and Levine, 1981), the two earlier periods corresponding
to the time of troubles immediately preceding and following the
World Wars. The most recent revival of interest in general
education followed the end of the Vietnam War, and the
curricular dissolution of the 1960s. The period from 1975 to the
present has been marked by a revival of interest in general
education and in restoring integrity to the undergraduate curriculum through recourse to core curricula and other strategies of
ensuring a broad general, and, in some cases, liberal education.
Gaff (1983: 207–20) lists over 300 American colleges and
universities which, at the time of his survey, were reviewing
general education.

Despite all the current interest in general education, there is
little agreement on what constitutes a viable general education
program for any given institution. The disagreements center on
questions of content, structure, process and implementation, and
range across the spectrum of curricular philosophies and institutional types. There is a coherent body of literature that questions
the advisability of general education in any form (Hall and
Kevles, 1982), and others believe that the assumptions of general
education, insofar as they are articulated at all, need to be
subjected to a radical criticism (Gros Louis, 1981).

The three twentieth-century revivals of general education
have focused on what might be called 'shared cultural values',
including notions of a common history, common political and
economic attitudes, common languages, and a common vision of
the future. During periods of world war and the economic
dislocation attendant on them, these common values became
'lost' or at least overshadowed by more pressing and immediate

problems of national survival, only to be regained with the return to better times that our national optimism assures us are imminent. This posture toward curricular change suggests that there is always something to go back to, that there is a common set of cultural artifacts we periodically recover and reaffirm through reinstituting general education programs which inculcate their values in college students. Such values were called into question, however, in the most recent fragmentation of the undergraduate curriculum that occurred in the milieu of the Vietnam War, the civil rights movement, and the student revolts of the 1960s.

Any attempt to recapture the unity of cultural values formerly expressed by general education curricula may be doomed to failure, however, if there is no longer any basis for asserting such unity. One might argue persuasively that the fragmentation of American society did not cause the collapse of common culture, but rather that the collapse of common culture caused the fragmentation of American society. Such a reversal, if true, would have important implications for general education since there is nothing to return to after collapse; nothing except the project of making a common culture anew, and of instituting the processes under which such a project might successfully be realized.

The critical theory of the contemporary German philosopher Jurgen Habermas (1971, 1975, 1979) is particularly helpful in analyzing both common cultural values, and the processes which form them. Habermas's critical theory aims at restoring the background consensus which is implicit in the processes of human discourse. Its aim is the liberation of human consciousness from the unnecessary restraints of ideologically rigidified and uncritically internalized human relations in whatever forms they may take – cultural, economic, pedagogical, political, and so on. The liberation is grounded in the communication process undertaken at both the .reflective level, where the rules for discourse are made, and at the unreflected level, where most discourse actually takes place. When we engage in criticism, we are announcing a position from which we view the reality criticized; that position itself may or may not have been critically formed or rationally discussed, and it may or may not be reflectively acknowledged in the course of the criticism. To the extent that it is uncritically accepted, it becomes an obstacle to cultural change, and a limit to freedom of thought and communication.

The fragmentation of the undergraduate curriculum and the dissolution of general education programs during the 1960s and 1970s may be seen as symptomatic of a larger cultural malaise only from a point of view that finds such fragmentation problematic, and that finds in the history of American higher education something of an original unity. Neither point of view, of course, is without certain philosophical presuppositions. The project of realizing curricular coherence must be preceded by a critical analysis of the philosophies of general education that have served to inform twentieth-century discussion. An examination of the articulated and hidden assumptions of the predominant philosophies of general education can facilitate a more rational, open, and authentic dialogue on their efficacy and utility in the reconstruction of the undergraduate curricula in general, and of general education programs in particular.

Gaff cites four distinctive philosophical approaches that ground the wide variety of general education models, proposals and polemics (1983: 2–8). Each approach has identifiable philosophical mentors and literatures, and each has its modern adherents and advocates.

(1) The first philosophical school is the Idealist School, founded by John Henry Newman (1873, 1947). Newman saw the college as a community of scholars whose primary function was teaching undergraduates in an atmosphere conducive to learning. The goal of a proper education was the liberation of the student from prejudice, ignorance and the provincialism of the immediate environment, but without the socially didactic emphasis characteristic of many of the other philosophical approaches. The traditional content of such a program, the humanities, had no specifically vocational purpose, but was rather designed to educate the whole person for all of life. Liberal education, for idealists like Newman, may or may not be synonymous with general education, but in the optimal case, it certainly would be.

(2) The Progressive School,[1] founded by philosophers Alfred North Whitehead (1929) and John Dewey (1916), has as its central tenet the notion that education must be relevant to the

student's everyday life. Today that means that education must be conceived from the point of view of the student. What is not relevant to the immediate present has credence only insofar as it can be made to shed light on the future. Utility is the watchword for these Progressives, a utility that is not altogether mundane – that which has no relevance to the student's immediate situation, has relevance to someone else's immediate situation and so is in some sense exploitive of what must be the ultimate arbiter of curricular matters, the student's interest.

(3) The Essentialist School of Robert Maynard Hutchins (1936) comes immediately to mind when one speaks of a core curriculum. The belief that there is a common and essential core of knowledge that every educated person should somehow 'possess' is the guiding principle behind the Essentialist creed. To the extent that there are essential texts that are relevant for all times and in all situations, the Essentialist argues for their use in the training of the mind, the goal of a general education. The Great Books program at the University of Chicago is perhaps the most widely known Essentialist approach to general education, although great books are not the only manifestation of the approach. Any approach that requires the mastery of an essential core of information or processes is philosophically akin to the Essentialist perspective. Thus Ernest Boyer, Martin Kaplan and Arthur Levine (1977, 1981) and most recently Alan Bloom (Bloom, 1987), are advocates of the Essentialist position, as are many others. There is a sense in which the Essentialist presuppositions are present in all programs of general education.

(4) The philosophical movement known as Pragmatism is normally associated with William James, but in the history of American higher education, the movement has contemporary voices in Clark Kerr (1982) and David Riesman (1981). This school recognizes the pluralistic character of American higher education, and celebrates it as a positive development indicative of a robust technological society. Kerr uses the term 'multiversity' to describe the environment of contemporary higher education, and its diverse student population. The Pragmatists advocate incremental changes that recognize the legitimate interests of the several communities that comprise the contemporary multiversity, and situational curricular reforms that fit the special and unique environments of individual institutions. The central tenet of Pragmatism is the realistic evaluation of the

possible, as opposed to ideal critique based on utopian visions.

Regardless of the form general education may take, the philosophical justification for the program calls on one or more of these four philosophies of education for its legitimation. The careful explication and critique of these philosophies is an over-riding concern, along with the explication of the hidden and acknowledged philosophical assumptions of general education. This work is also concerned to develop a critical perspective from which to evaluate these philosophical assumptions using the critical theory of Habermas (1971, 1975, 1979), and to judge the extent to which the various assumptions are vitiated or confirmed by the developed critical theory.

Jonas Soltis (1984) has tried to put all of the current research methodologies in education into a coherent conceptual framework utilizing the work of Richard Bernstein (1978) as a guide to their epistemological histories. In so doing, Soltis develops three categories of contemporary educational inquiry that are borrowed from Habermas: the empirical, the interpretive, and the critical.

Empirical inquiry employs natural science methodology from 'naturalistic descriptions, survey data gathering, and correlation studies to control-treatment experiments and meta-analyses of empirical findings' (Soltis, 1984: 6). Empirical inquiry is fundamentally quantitative, and employs the language of logical empiricism; though there are many different interpretations of what constitutes a true science among its adherents, and there are many contradictions between what passes muster as proper procedure in theory, and what is actually practiced. Nevertheless, there seems to be a naïve consensus that educational research ought to be empirical, objective (though there are conflicting definitions and standards for objectivity) and essentially value free.

Interpretive inquiry, by contrast, is qualitative rather than quantitative, and depends on the methodologies of such disciplines as anthropology, sociolinguistics and ethnography to direct value-free inquiry into the realm of intersubjective meanings. Ordinary language analysis, phenomenology, and hermeneutics, the social science equivalents of interpretive inquiry, investigate human intersubjective meanings as keys to the relationships between education and culture. The interpretive approach insists on an understanding of the ways in which human consciousness operates in and upon the world. The study of human consciousness, in turn, presents special methodological problems since that which is investigating is also that which is being investigated, and therefore the investigation is not purely 'objective' from the point of view of empirical science.

Critical inquiry, the third research methodology, has an ideological content that is specifically recognized, even celebrated, and that sees other methodologies as ideological moments in the unfolding of human experience. The notion of a value-free science is, to such scholars, an expression of the denial of the unity of theory and practice, and itself an ideological form of inquiry. The object of critical inquiry is the realization of a better form of life that serves our emancipatory interests. The critical scholars emphasize the historical-ideological content of our present institutions in an attempt to demystify them and make them more responsive to the people and ideals they serve.

All three methods of educational research are necessary and desirable elements of the associated community of which we are all part. No one scholar can do all three, but all scholars have an interest in seeing all three done properly, and all scholars have an interest in seeing the gulf between theory and practice, between what ought to be and what is, appreciably diminished.

The methodological approaches described above are borrowed from Bernstein (1978), who interprets the philosophy of Habermas (1971). In Habermas' philosophy, the tension between theory and practice plays a major role in the development of a critical theory of society. The project of the Frankfurt School, to which Habermas is heir, was to develop a critical theory of society that took as its starting point the critique of logical positivism (Jay, 1973). In an age of technology, the practical (that is, the ethically and morally desirable), tends to be proscribed by the objectively possible such that the technically possible, and perhaps only the technically possible, ought to be desired. Politics, for example, is no longer the classical extension of the good life, a continuation of ethics, but rather a science – the science of the possible. What is technically possible is done, and what is not technically possible is not only not done, but is not the object of 'rational' desire either.

So the problem for the modern social scientists, as Bernstein points out (1978: 186–7), is how to reconcile the practical and the technical in a way that sacrifices neither. How can the 'good life' be defined in terms of its own internal necessity and at the same time within the context of the technically (objectively) possible? If the logic of technological rationality is dominant in our culture – that is, if instrumental reason is the dominant form of reason, and if all other forms of reason (critical and individual) are insufficient to the standards of instrumentality and therefore to some extent 'irrational' from the point of view of the dominant logic – then how is criticism of the dominant culture possible? Where do the social theorists, of whom the educational researcher may be one, stand when they address the status quo? And what methodology do they employ?

Habermas argues that instrumental reason is indeed the dominant form of reason in contemporary society and that

> . . . the relationship of theory to praxis can now only assert itself as the purposive-rational application of techniques assured by empirical science. The social potential of science is reduced to the powers of technical control – its potential for enlightened action is no longer considered. The empirical, analytical sciences produce technical recommendations, but they furnish no answer to practical questions. (Habermas, 1973: 254)

In a culture where the control of nature is also the control of human nature, and where the techniques necessary for that task are in place, questions of practical import tend to be reduced to questions of technical application. Rational consensus is replaced by efficient administration whose legitimating power is technological rationality.

A scientistic interpretation of epistemology results in an epistemology in which all knowledge is measured by the standards of an empirical and objective science. Such an epistemology ignores the connection between knowledge and what Habermas calls 'human interests' (1971: 301–17). It ignores, put simply, the fact that the questions one asks of nature determine the answers one hears from nature, and that the method of science is not itself at all disinterested. The project Habermas launches details the process by which reason becomes self-conscious; that is, how self-reflection (one hears the Socratic dictum to 'know thyself') becomes the foundation for a critical theory of society. In doing this, he analyzes the three forms of cognitive interests that human consciousness takes, and shows how each is appropriate to a particular science and a particular dimension of human social existence. These three cognitive interests correspond to the methods of educational research suggested by Soltis.

Human cognitive interests (see definitions p. 117) are exclusively determined neither by an organism's interaction with its environment, nor by pure rational thought, but rather by the interaction of both in the act of reproduction and self-affirmation of the species. Habermas focuses upon three basic cognitive interests: the technical, the practical, and the emancipatory. Each of the three interests is reflected in a corresponding human science: for the technical interest, the empirical-analytic sciences; for the practical interest, historical-hermeneutic sciences; and for the emancipatory interest, the critically-oriented sciences. The dimensions of human social existence upon which the cognitive interests are grounded are, correspondingly, work, interaction, and power.

Technical interest, which is rooted in work as the fundamental human activity, is primarily concerned with how individuals reproduce themselves materially, through manipulating their environment. Such activity is both social and individual; it results in the perpetuation of both the species and the individual member of the species. The tension that exists between what satisfies species' existence and that which at any particular time satisfies individual existence but violates species' existence, is inherent in the dynamic character of the relationship between work as social and as individual activity. The cognitive interest involved in satisfying material needs incorporates instrumental action governed by technical rules, the object of which is the efficient manipulation of·the environment for the satisfaction of human needs. The technical rules for the manipulation of the environment are based on empirical knowledge and involve predictions (Habermas, 1971). Technical control over the environment is made possible by the rigorous application of rationally derived and empirically verified rules, and the continuous investigation into that which is unknown.

Practical interest, which is rooted in interaction, is distinguished from the technical interest which is rooted in work in that

> . . . the meaning of the validity of propositions is not consti-
> tuted in the frame of reference of technical control. . . . Access
> to the facts is provided by the understanding of meaning, not
> observation. (Habermas, 1971: 309)

The interpretation of texts, hermeneutics, has its own set of
socially accepted and verified rules based on the interest in
establishing an intersubjective realm rooted in consensus. As
with the empirical-analytical sciences, the historical-hermeneutic
sciences have a context from which they inquire into reality, and
that context colors the results of their inquiry no less than the
context of the individual empirical scientist colors his. In the
empirical-analytic sciences the danger is scientism, in the
historical-hermeneutic sciences, historicism. Both dangers are
rooted in the intentional nature of human consciousness by
which it projects itself into the inquiry by which it seeks to
understand reality. We re-write the history of the French
Revolution every generation not because the 'facts' have
changed, but because the meaning which we attribute to them
has been reshaped by our future intentions, and because we
implicitly acknowledge the possibility of reaching a consensus
concerning our visions of the future. The aim here is not control
and manipulation, but establishing and reaffirming the conditions for authentic forms of intersubjectivity.

Emancipatory interest, which is rooted in the critical social
sciences, aims at a different level of knowledge from the nomological knowledge which is sought by the empirical-analytic
historical-hermeneutic sciences. The critical social sciences are
concerned with going beyond the goal of nomological knowledge
to

> . . . determine when theoretical statements grasp invariant
> regularities of social action as such and when they express
> ideologically frozen relations of dependence that can in prin-
> ciple be transformed. (Habermas, 1971: 310)

The reflexive nature of human consciousness allows consciousness to take itself as an object of reflection, but that reflection is
colored by the facticity of the situation that called it forth in the
first place. The critique of ideology on the social level has
psychoanalysis as its counterpart on the individual level – the

desired result is emancipation of the unreflected levels of social and individual consciousness through self-reflection. Metaphorically speaking, the same critical distance provided to the patient by the analyst is provided to society by the critical theorist, with the same risks and provisos, and the same demands for authentic communication.

Without general education there is no ground in which we find the common elements of discourse within the undergraduate curriculum. This does not mean that there is no common ground for discourse; it means that the ground is unarticulated, and therefore uncriticized, and consequently outside the realm of reflective consciousness. General education, at least potentially, brings within the purview of critical reason the unexamined elements of individual and collective consciousness that constitute, through daily application, the fabric of our cultural lives.

In an advanced technological society, reason itself has become a tool used to realize the goals one holds at any given time (Horkheimer, 1974). Instrumental reason is reason directed at defined ends and propelled by the logic of efficiency. It assumes that nature and man are manipulable and transparent to human purposes, and that any other form of human thought not dictated by the logic of efficiency is outside the realm of reason and therefore irrational. The problem is to determine the extent to which instrumental reason distorts the communicative processes necessary for the formulation of a critical theory of general education. Metaphorically speaking, one could say that instrumental reason is to general education what ideology is to culture, insofar as both instrumental reason and ideology are legitimating forces for established ways of doing things.

What follows is an attempt to provide a theoretical ground from which further empirical research may be conducted by explicating the critical theory of Jurgen Habermas and by making it accessible to curricular reformers. An authentic dialogue concerning the philosophical roots of general education will frame a context for other curricular reform.

Note

1. Here the term 'Progressive' is applied to the philosophy of John Dewey and his followers, while the term 'Pragmatism' is applied to the

philosophy of education that appears in the work of Clark Kerr. John Dewey was a member of the American philosophical movement known as Pragmatism, but his educational philosophy was part of the political movement known as Progressivism. To avoid confusion I refer to Dewey's educational philosophy as 'Progressivism'.

1 Theories of General Education

IDEALISM

The four approaches to general education, Idealism, Progress-ivism, Essentialism, and Pragmatism are explicated in this chapter. These approaches to general education fall into a chronology that begins in the mid-nineteenth century and ends in the present debates, but they are not exhaustive of all possible variations and combinations of specific general educational programs throughout American curricular history. Nevertheless, the philosophical presuppositions of these approaches are pres-ent in all general education programs in one form or another, and it is the presuppositions, sometimes articulated and criti-cized, sometimes hidden and assumed, that are the concern of this work.

Historical Background

John Henry Cardinal Newman was an Englishman, educated at Oxford, and one of the major proponents of the forces of religious orthodoxy at that institution during the first half of the nine-teenth century. He converted to Catholicism in October of 1845 and asked to be dropped from the rolls of Oxford that same year. His conversion and his defection from Oxford can be understood as an affirmation of the values of the older and now dying tradition of education wherein religion played a central role. Newman always held that education was more properly the training of minds and the forming of character than it was the imparting, much less the discovery, of new information in the sense of the new sciences. Religion, obviously, played a central role, one which he was to argue forcibly in *The Idea of A University*, written in 1851.

But in 1845 the population of Ireland was approximately 8.5 million, of whom 7 million were Roman Catholic and 0.75 million were Anglican. Higher education was provided only to the Anglican minority, however, since an act of formal apostasy was required for the admission of all Catholics to the University of Dublin, the only institution of higher education in Ireland at the time (Culler, 1955: 124). The political situation became volatile during the 1840s when O'Connell and the Young Ireland Party were agitating for repeal of the Union at the same time the United States had engaged England in a possible military confrontation over the Oregon territories. This combination of circumstances led to a policy of conciliation on the part of the English government, the result of which was the Queen's College Scheme.

The Queen's College Scheme embraces the principle that public education must be neutral – especially with regard to religion, and that, in order to be neutral, it must be thoroughly secular. This amounted to 'mixed education', that is, the educating of students of all religious persuasions in the same institution and at the same time, a notion whose time had not yet come in Ireland, and a notion to which Newman was unalterably opposed. A compromise proposal that would establish colleges of university standing in several communities, while leaving the University of Dublin unchanged, these Queen's Colleges were soon dubbed by their detractors the 'Godless Colleges', and the opinion was, as were most opinions in the Ireland of the day, divided to say the least (Culler, 1955: 123–30). But following the great potato famine of 1845, all proposals emanating from England were critically scrutinized.

This reluctance to accept English proposals, combined with a great reluctance to take a chance on mixed education, held the issue in abeyance for the two years it took the Catholic Church to reach a decision on the propriety of the Queen's Colleges. That decision came in October of 1847, and while it was not viewed by the Irish clergy as final, it most strongly disapproved of the notion of mixed education in the colleges, and ordered the Catholic prelates to take no part in them. It is in this context that Newman, in 1851, was asked by Dr Cullen, Archbishop of Armagh and Primate of All Ireland, to give a few lectures regarding the nature of education generally and the proper role of the university particularly. The lectures were to be given in the face of the strong possibility that a Catholic institution of higher education might soon be founded. The lectures were originally known as the 'Discourses on University Education', and later as *The Idea of A University* (Newman, 1947: originally published 1873).

The 'Discourses' deal with two basic questions, and the ancillary questions surrounding them. The first question, and the one most prominently featured in the popular debates on the nature of the Irish university, was whether a university was the proper place for the teaching of theology. Newman held that it was, of course, but for different reasons than might be argued by a purely sectarian advocacy. These arguments constitute the core of the first four discourses and the last two. The second question, which is answered in the remaining discourses, concerns the objects of knowledge and their utilitarian applications.

These were the questions of the age, and their satisfactory resolution determines the line of demarcation between Idealism and the utilitarian philosophies of Mill and, in America, Dewey and the Progressives. Should the university focus its teaching on the special studies which have immediate practical application, or should it focus on those studies which improve and develop the mind? The question is really one of whether truth is validated by correspondence theory (that is, by an investigation of the connection between the mind and its objects, in this case an empirical investigation), or coherence theory (that is, by an investigation of the rational, logical and aesthetic coherence of the mind and its ideas). Newman came down firmly on the side of coherence. In fact, for Newman, the recombination of the distinct sciences, the reconstitution of the whole from which they are abstracted, is the major task of the university.

Newman's idealism is a cultural idealism in which he attempts to synthesize existing knowledge into a coherent whole that illuminates a reality whose constituent parts are knowable to finite minds only as fragments of a larger whole. The fragmentation of knowledge gives the illusion of control, it makes knowledge synonymous with power; more knowledge means more power. But, as Newman clearly sees, this fragmentation also does violence to man's understanding of himself as part of a larger whole for which modern thought no longer has proper reverence. To this extent, Newman's work is an attempt to rectify the excesses of the scientific age, and it is ironic that the university he finally helped to found bore such little resemblance to his own ideal.

The Ideal University

The view taken of a University in these discourses is the following: That it is a place of *teaching* and universal *knowledge*. This implies that its object is, on the one hand, intellectual, not moral: and, on the other, that it is the diffusion and extension of knowledge rather than the advancement. If its object were scientific and philosophical discovery, I do not see why a University should have students; if religious training, I do not see how it can be the seat of literature and science. (Newman, 1912: ix)

In the preface to the Discourses, Newman notes that the university in its essence, and without the Church, has the above characteristics. But it cannot fulfill this mission without the Church because it needs the Church for its integrity. So when the Pope called for the establishment of an Irish university, he was calling not for the importation of the English university onto Irish soil, but for the formation of a uniquely Irish institution that addressed uniquely Irish problems. This meant, in part, that the Irish youth be educated at least as well as their English counterparts in the instrumental skills necessary to compete in the world of men, but more, that Irish youth be educated into 'culture of the intellect'. The 'culture of the intellect' is the

. . . force, the steadiness, the comprehensiveness and the versatility of intellect, the command over our own powers, the instinctive just estimate of things as they pass before us . . . (Newman, 1947: xvi)

The mind is like the body, it needs to be disciplined, formed carefully so that it develops a connected view or grasp of the world. For this kind of education, the Irish university would be peculiarly suited, in part because the functions of teaching and research ought to be clearly distinguished, the latter having no proper place in the university (Newman, 1947: xiii). This frees the faculty from the division of attention characteristic of research oriented institutions, and at the same time remains consonant with the avowed coherence theory of truth that is the epistemological foundation for Newman's idealism.

This is not to say, however, that Newman is open to the charge that his educational theory will produce students of vacuous and general knowledge, for while these discourses concern the aims, rather than the modes of education, nevertheless,

> ... I hold very strongly that the first step in intellectual training is to impress upon a boy's mind the idea of science, method, order, principle, and system; of rule and exception, of richness and harmony. (Newman, 1947: xix)

In other words, Newman advocates at least study *about* science, if not the real thing itself. He goes on to advocate the study of Grammar and Mathematics (to give the student a 'conception of development and arrangement from and around a common centre'), Chronology and Geography, which are necessary to read History, as well as Metrical Composition necessary to read Poetry (Newman, 1947: xix).

In the first and introductory discourse, Newman is concerned to provide some sort of ground for his discussions. He feels the tension between faith and reason, but more he feels the tension between religion and instrumentalism. He knows that the education provided by Protestant institutions has a practical advantage over that proposed by the Pope in the new Catholic university, but Newman argues that the practical advantages of a secular education are not comparable to the intellectual advantages of a Catholic education. Newman remains true to the principles of Catholicism and the wishes of the Holy See, but he nevertheless seeks to legitimize his arguments by appealing to the history of the English university and the dictates of common sense.

> Let it be observed, then, that the principles on which I would conduct the inquiry are attainable . . . by the mere experience of life. They do not come simply by theology; they imply no supernatural discernment; they have no special connection with Revelation; they almost arise out of the nature of the case; they are dictated even by human prudence and wisdom, though a divine illumination be absent, and they are recognized by common sense, even where self-interest is not

present to quicken it; and, therefore, though true, and just, and good in themselves, they imply nothing whatever as to the religious profession of those who maintain them. They may be held by Protestants as well as by Catholics; nay, there is reason to anticipate that in certain times and places they will be more thoroughly investigated, and better understood, and held more firmly by Protestants than by ourselves. (Newman, 1947: 5)

Catholics, Newman argues, have been sheltered from the storm by their faith, and Protestants, as a consequence, are better equipped to deal with the 'science of education'. For them knowledge is power and nothing else, but for the Catholics who have been protected by a special spiritual coherence, the 'science of education' is new ground. So Newman proceeds by the force of the better agument as determined by human reason and focused by human wisdom.

Theology and the Proper Role of the University

Since the Queen's College Scheme proposed the effective exclusion of theology as an academic discipline from the university curriculum, Newman is compelled to deal with the issue of the proper relation between theology and the university. In doing so he advocates the inclusion of theology as an academic discipline, and develops a curricular epistemology based upon a rational and ideal conception of the nature of human knowledge.

If a university, as its name implies, ought to teach universal knowledge, and Theology is a branch of that knowledge, then it follows syllogistically that a university ought to teach theology. The argument assumes that the university teaches universal knowledge, an assumption not shared by all parties to the dispute, and it also assumes that theology is a legitimate branch of human knowledge, an assumption that the epistemology of the time was beginning to question. These assumptions are not hidden. Newman makes them explicit in the introductory passages, and they are not unexamined; but Newman is an Englishman and a recent convert to Catholicism, and is arguing before Irishmen who have been Catholic since the beginning of time. He argues simply that religion and theology are a part of the human experience, and they ought to be accorded at least as much importance as those other parts of the human experience included in the university curricula. His argument is generic at this point, he is not arguing for Catholic theology as opposed to Protestant or Anglican theology, he is merely arguing that Theology, as a legitimate field of human inquiry, ought to be included in the curricula because to exclude it would be to exclude an essential element of human knowledge, and therefore render the institution less than universal in its scope.

> In word, indeed, and in idea, it is easy enough to divide Knowledge into human and divine, secular and religious, and to lay down that we will address ourselves to the one without interfering with the other; but it is impossible in fact. Granting that divine truth differs in kind from human, so do human truths differ in kind one from another. If the knowledge of the Creator is in a different order from knowledge of the creature, so, in like manner, metaphysical science is in a different order from physical, physics from history, history from ethics. You will soon break up into fragments the whole circle of secular knowledge, if you begin the mutilation with the divine. (Newman 1947: 16)

The relations among the different disciplines, among the different dimensions of human knowledge, hinge on the way in which truth is conceived. For Newman, truth is the object of knowledge of whatever kind; it has to do with facts and their relations, 'which stand toward each other pretty much as subjects and predicates in logic' (Newman, 1947: 45). The truth forms a continuous whole, whose parts are defined by human conviction, and from the point of view of the whole (from the divine point of view) those conventions are arbitrary. There is one reality, one whole, one ideal cosmos, that is apprehended by human consciousness only partially and inadequately. The human mind can never take it all in at one glance, or ever 'possess' any sense of the whole complex of relationships defined by the various sciences. The sciences are partial views, abstractions, by means of which human consciousness penetrates the various aspects of a single reality, and they are 'true' so far as they go.

The truth of human knowledge about the world, for Newman, is contingent upon the mastery of the various partial views, upon the mastery of the sciences. The sciences are interdependent, they are the results of mental processes directed at one reality, and consequently human knowledge is adequate only insofar as it embraces the range of the sciences in their interrelatedness.

> Viewed altogether, they approximate to a representation or subjective reflection of the objective truth, as nearly as is possible to the human mind, which advances towards the accurate apprehension of that object, in proportion to the number of sciences which it has mastered . . . (Newman, 1947: 47)

Newman is not saying that knowledge is merely additive, but rather that knowledge is knowledge of something *Ideal*, and is therefore always and everywhere incomplete. Human beings can approximate universal knowledge only at the species level, so what Newman argues is proper for a university to teach, might not be possible for an individual to know.

Newman reserves a special role for philosophy as the science of the sciences, that branch of knowledge that synthesizes the parts into a coherent whole. Philosophy analyzes the limitations of each of the sciences, their relations one to another, and their relations to the whole. Theology, on the other hand, is defined by Newman as the 'Science of God' (1947: 61); the truths that it is possible for man to know about God put into some sort of rational system, so that the parts are coherent in the human understanding. The God Newman conceives is the life principle that lies behind the veil of the visible universe and acts through it much as the human life principle lies behind the visible manifestations of the human world and acts through it. These conceptions are far from clear. There is a sense in which Theology is inferior to Philosophy when Newman conceptualizes human knowledge as a hierarchy, and a sense in which Philosophy stands outside the sciences when Newman characterizes them as a 'circle of sciences'. Nevertheless, it is clear that Newman conceives human knowledge as interrelated, so that no one part can be neglected without doing violence to all the rest. Each has its special vision, each its power to illuminate a part of the whole; the neglect of any one science results in a shadowy and fragmentary and therefore untrustworthy understanding of the others.

Thus far Newman has been considering the bearing of theology on the other branches of knowledge. He now turns the inquiry around and considers the bearing of the other branches of knowledge on theology, with essentially the same results. The exclusive cultivation of any of the sciences results in impoverished understanding of the truth, that truth seen as the apprehension of the Ideal whole (which, we must remember, is really outside the capacity of any particular individual). The perception of truth is further clouded by the exclusive application of one science because the legitimate boundaries of that science are soon breached and it encroaches on territory not its own, and attempts the solution of problems for which it has no proper instruments (Newman, 1947: 74). This instrumental objection to the extension of the sciences into realms (such as the theological) where they are inadequate to the task, obviates the moral argument that the sciences ought not encroach on areas of divine revelation by making the encroachment by biology on theology of a kind with the encroachment of biology on any other science. Yet it is common, even inevitable, that men are called upon to speak and act outside their narrow disciplines about things of which they know little. In such instances, the danger is that they have little trouble deciding, and usually deciding wrongly and, at the time, quite convincingly.

This leads Newman to his major objection for the exclusion of theology from the curriculum.

> . . . it is not only the loss of Theology, it is the perversion of other sciences. What it unjustly forfeits, others unjustly seize. They have their own department, and, in going out of it, attempt to do what they really cannot do; and that the more mischievously, because they do teach what in its place is true, though when out of its place, perverted or carried to excess, it is not true. And, as every man has not the capacity of separating truth from falsehood, they persuade the world of what is false by urging upon it what is true. (Newman, 1947: 78)

Furthermore, a man who has never studied theology may stray unwittingly into matters of theological dispute and never be aware of it. He has no 'landmarks' to guide his inquiries and to measure his life. There is a sense in which Newman and Plato are quite close insofar as they both see evil as a function of ignorance. The man who does not know the boundaries of the sciences, and the instruments appropriate to them, may indeed do evil and socially destructive things as he wanders and bumbles through life. Such a man has no awareness that there is a background consensus against which inquiries are properly conducted. He is unaware that the consensus is socially developed, often at great cost, by those interested in Truth. He cannot even communicate his deficiencies because he does not see them.

It was apparent to Newman that the unity of knowledge had been lost. In his view, it was to be the function of the university to restore the integrity of all knowledge, to seek after its unity and to reflect upon it. The loss of unity was due to the increasingly popular notion that knowledge was power, and that more knowledge was more power in a purely instrumental sense. The most efficient way to produce more knowledge had its parallel in the industrial model: the division of labor. This intellectual division of labor gave rise to the division of the sciences, and to the popular notion that all knowledge could be arbitrarily divided according to human convention. One of the most appalling developments of the time, and according to Culler one of the most troublesome popular attitudes with which Newman had to deal (Culler, 1955: 174), was the notion that all of human knowledge could be divided alphabetically and arranged in volumes for popular consumption. Encyclopedias were originally cyclical, that is, unified; their fragmentation according to the dictates of the alphabet reflected the loss of that unity which the original cyclical organization had implied.

If what was needed was not more knowledge, but the effective synthesis of all existing knowledge, then the relation between Knowledge and Utility needed clarification. This Newman proceeded to do in his Discourses V, VI, and VII.

Knowledge, Utility and the Role of the University

> I have said that all branches of knowledge are connected together, because the subject-matter of knowledge is intimately united in itself, as being the acts and the work of the Creator. Hence it is that the Sciences, into which our

knowledge may be said to be cast, have multiplied bearings one on another, and an internal sympathy, and admit, or rather demand, comparison and adjustment. They complete, correct, balance each other. (Newman, 1947: 99)

All sciences are inadequate by themselves, without the corrective perspectives of the others. The knowledge they impart is particular, uninformed by a global view, and insofar as utility determines the value of the particular sciences, their true ends are occluded. The particular sciences are necessary for the true ends of University education (which Newman calls variously Liberal or Philosophical Knowledge) for without them university education would have no content, no anchor in the world. But the end of university education cannot be separated from knowledge itself, for knowledge is its own end. 'Such is the constitution of the human mind, that any kind of knowledge, if it be really such, is its own reward' (Newman, 1947: 103). If this be true of the particular sciences, it is even more true of the Science of Sciences, Philosophy. The acquisition of this kind of knowledge satisfies a deep and abiding need in human nature.

The Liberal Knowledge (or Philosophical Knowledge), which satisfies such a human need, is knowledge which

. . . stands on its own pretensions, which is independent of sequel, expects no complement, refuses to be informed . . . by any end, or absorbed into any art, in order duly to present itself to our contemplation. (Newman, 1947: 108)

Newman's ideas are thoroughly Aristotelian, particularly with regard to his definitions of useful and liberal knowledge, which he quotes directly from Aristotle's *Rhetoric*. Those things that bear fruit and yield revenue are useful, those which lead to enjoyment and accrue nothing of consequence beyond their using are liberal (Newman, 1947: 109). Knowledge, to be liberal, must have no use beyond itself, that is, it must be philosophical in the sense that it relates to the interconnectedness of particular knowledge. As it becomes more utilitarian, as it becomes tied more intimately to a particular end, it ceases to be knowledge. Newman argues against a utilitarian standard for knowledge, which is consonant with his coherence theory of truth.

> Liberal Education, viewed in itself, is simply the cultivation of the intellect, as such, and its object is nothing more or less than intellectual excellence. (Newman, 1947: 121)

When Newman considers knowledge in relation to learning, Philosophy, Philosophical Knowledge, Enlargement of the Mind and Illumination, all become terms synonymous with the perfection or virtue of the intellect. The university, considered prior to its use as a tool of the Church (which it will certainly become for Newman), has as its end the perfection of the intellect. As such its object is to educate the intellect in proper reasoning and expose it to established truths. But the particular truths are inferior to the larger truths to which philosophy leads. Knowledge, in the sense of wisdom, transcends the narrow confines of specificity; the contents of the several sciences, while important prerequisites for knowledge, are not Knowledge in the larger sense. The mere communication of factual knowledge is methodologically necessary but not by itself sufficient to accomplish the ends of university education.

> The enlargement consists, not merely in the passive reception into the mind of a number of ideas hitherto unknown to it, but in the mind's energetic and simultaneous action upon and towards and among those new ideas, which are rushing in upon it. It is the action of a formative power, reducing to order and meaning the matter of our acquirements; it is a making the objects of our knowledge subjectively our own, or to use a familiar word, it is a digestion of what we receive, into the substance of our previous state of thought; and without this no enlargement is said to follow. (Newman, 1947: 133)

There is no enlargement, Newman argues, unless the mind compares ideas one with another and systematizes them by referring them to what it knows already. If it does not know anything, if there is nothing with which to compare and into which to systematize, the mind is not rooted, it has no point of view from which to launch itself, or at least the point of view it has is accidental and inadequate. Newman does not discuss how this process is initiated from birth, but it is clear that he is not sympathetic to the tabula rasa theory of learning, at least insofar as that theory leads to a passive conception of mind. To this extent his thought has a familiar modern ring. The great intellect, the one to which all ought aspire, is that which takes a connected view of reality, one in which the object is to understand rather than to manipulate, to know inquisitively, rather than acquisitively:

> . . . the true and adequate end of intellectual training and of a University is not Learning or Acquirement, but rather, is Thought or Reason exercised upon Knowledge, or what may be called Philosophy . . . . (Newman, 1947: 139)

Newman's conception calls for the generalist, the theorist, the seeker after roots and first principles, the global and encyclopedic mind.

Knowledge is additive. One who would aspire to philosophical knowledge, would apply oneself diligently to the distinct sciences, mastering their content and comparing and synthesizing their particular insights into nature as one proceeds. Newman must argue this way, because the only other way that he sees to achieve enlightenment is through an intuitive insight which he seeks to avoid because of the difficulty of reconciling such intuition with his coherence theory of truth. One must build systematically and in a disciplined fashion from ignorance to a more or less adequate notion of the whole – a rather large order for a university, an impossible one for an individual.

Having shown that liberal knowledge or liberal education is education for itself, without an end beyond itself, Newman now proceeds to show that it also has a curious utility, if by utility we mean

> . . . not what is simply good, but what *tends* to good, or is the *instrument* of good; and in this sense also . . . I will show you how a liberal education is truly and fully a useful, though it be not a professional, education. (Newman, 1947: 163, 164)

Professional education, is not the *sufficient* end of a university education, though it might not be excluded from a university curriculum (indeed, Newman founded a medical school at the Catholic University of Ireland). The irony is that while the individual sciences are undoubtedly advanced by specialization, the individual scientist is often retarded thereby, particularly if the special utility of a liberal education is lost in the advance of the scientific and specialized knowledge of the scientist. Liberal education facilitates the proper discharge of the individual's obligations to society, it makes him a better, more productive and happier citizen, not to mention a more prudent Christian.

> If then a practical end must be assigned to a University course, I say it is that of training good members of society. Its art is the art of social life, and its end is fitness for the world. It neither confines its views to particular professions on the one hand, nor creates heroes or inspires genius on the other. Works of genius fall under no art; heroic minds come under no rule; a University is not a birthplace of poets or of immortal authors, of founders of schools, leaders of colonies, or conquerors of nations . . . But a University training aims at raising the intellectual tone of society, at cultivating the public mind, at purifying the national taste, at supplying true principles to popular enthusiasm and fixed aims to popular aspirations, at giving enlargement and sobriety to the ideas of the age, at facilitating the exercise of political power, and refining the intercourse of private life. (Newman 1947: 177, 178)

In this and passages of a similar tone, Newman sounds very much like certain advocates of general education in the twentieth century. The program might vary in specific content, and certainly in the theological tone with which Newman imbues his philosophy, but there is nevertheless a set of assumptions at work in both.

Principles and Assumptions of Newman's Idealism

– While scientific truths may be discovered inductively, philosophical truth is validated through the logical coherence of its propositions.
– Finite minds do not know philosophical truth through an intuitive grasp of the whole of reality, but through an additive process by which they build an ideal and logically coherent truth.
– Knowledge (truth) is not synonymous with power, that is, Newman's conception of knowledge and truth is ideal, not instrumental, and while truths may have instrumental benefits

which are incidental to them, the danger of instrumental reason is that it reifies knowledge, making it a thing capable of both possession and manipulation.

– The mind can (and needs to be) 'disciplined' and 'formed' so that it develops a connected view of things. The absence of a connected view is the source of much evil. In this respect, Newman is Platonic: evil is a function of ignorance.

– The mind, while capable of being formed and disciplined, is nevertheless not passive, but active.

– Knowledge is both hierarchical and circular. Newman speaks of both a hierarchy of knowledge, with philosophy at its pinacle (and informed by the Catholic faith), and of a circle of sciences where philosophy is the science of sciences.

– Excessive specialization in any one of the sciences, while advancing the science, retards the individual scientist and leads to an impoverished understanding of the connectedness of things.

– The university is a place of teaching and universal knowledge whose object is intellectual, not moral; its object is the diffusion and dissemination of knowledge, not its advancement. This implies that there is and ought to be a pedagogical distinction between teaching and research.

– The true end of the university is liberal or philosophical knowledge which is its own end.

PROGRESSIVISM

Historical Background

John Dewey's productive life spanned the years from 1882, when he published his first article ('The Metaphysical Assumptions of Materialism'), to his death in 1952. He was prolific throughout his entire life; always the philosopher in process, constantly changing and revising his views, adapting to a world that was undergoing transformations of epochal proportions. His thought, therefore, changes as dramatically from the late nineteenth century to the middle of the twentieth as the world of which it was a clear, if peculiarly American, expression.

Hahn (1970) divides Dewey's work into three periods reflecting his metaphysical point of view. Early in his career Dewey was heavily influenced by Kant and intuitionalism, arguing forcibly against the materialist metaphysics which denied intuition, and in favor of religion and values. Later, as a graduate student, Dewey discovered Hegel, and adapted Hegel's idealism to the experimentalism of the 1890s, and eventually to the instrumentalism that gave way, in his mature phase, to 'empirical naturalism, or pragmatic naturalism, or contextualism' (Hahn, 1970: 16). Dewey's thought was thus influenced by the major thinkers of the eighteenth and nineteenth centuries, and represented an attempt to ground philosophy in ordinary experience, while at the same time maintaining the integrity of the discipline. Human values, for example, were to become, for Dewey, part of a reconstructive reflective inquiry in which dualisms were imploded, rather than the expressions of a transcendent reality on the one hand, or of an absolute spirit making itself manifest through time, on the other. The recognition that the human intellect acts in an interested way in the world did not mean, for Dewey, that philosophy was impossible; but it did mean that philosophy as traditionally practiced – as the 'quest for certainty' – would have to be abandoned, and a new and more vital motivation substituted in its place. The question of the nature of that motivation, the idea that human motivation can be, and indeed often is, utterly perverse, was foreign to Dewey's optimism and places his thought in the 'pre-Holocaust' period of bourgeois philosophy.

Dewey's Quest for Certainty

In *The Quest for Certainty* (1960; originally published 1929), Dewey articulated the role of philosophy for the Progressive age, a role that rehabilitated the material against the ideal, and the practical against the purely intellectual. The hazardous and fragile nature of human existence forces man to seek security in two ways: by appeasing the gods, and by developing the tools to master the environment. In the first way, man attempts to change his 'self', that is, his emotional and spiritual nature, and to bring it into line with the powers of an inhospitable fate; in the second, he attempts to change the world through action in and upon it. The tension between these two ways of confronting the reality of human temporality are part of the history of the species, and can best be expressed by wondering at whether the invention of tools offends and invades the prerogatives of the gods, and thereby further endangers an already insecure future. The estrangement of theory from practice is rooted in the cultural traditions of Western man, and is justified by philosophy as necessary to preserve the sacred from contamination by the mundane. In fact, the mundane matters of life are better left to the care of a slave class, whenever possible, and at any rate are never to be elevated to the status of matters of intellect, matters suited to a leisured and educated aristocracy. At least, Dewey argues, so it was in Greek society, where the life of the *polis* was carried out by the intellectual élite, on the backs of an unlettered and devalued populace.

> The depreciation of action, of doing and making, has been cultivated by philosophers. But while philosophers have perpetuated the derogation by formulating and justifying it, they did not originate it. They glorified their own office without doubt in placing theory so much above practice. But independently of their attitude, many things conspired to the same effect. Work has been onerous, toilsome, associated with a primeval curse. It has been done under compulsion and the pressure of necessity, while intellectual activity is associated with leisure. On account of the unpleasantness of practical activity, as much of it as possible has been put upon slaves and serfs. Thus the social dishonor in which this class was held was extended to the work they do. (Dewey, 1929: 4, 5)

The cause of such an attitude is tied to the quest for certainty which in turn recognizes the inherently uncertain nature of practical activity in all its forms. As man struggles to survive the vagaries of material deprivation, he recognizes himself as tenuous, as an inessential and fleeting moment in an uncertain scenario.

Man seeks self-transcendence as a way to anchor himself in the face of change and uncertainty. Change and uncertainty infect everything man *does*, so he attempts to avoid doing in favor of thinking, in favor of *contemplation* in the Aristotelian sense.

> The quest for certainty is a quest for a peace which is assured, an object which is unqualified by risk and the shadow of fear which action casts . . . quest for complete certainty can be

fulfilled in pure knowledge alone. Such is the verdict of our most enduring philosophic tradition. (Dewey, 1929: 8)

Modern man, of course, has surrounded himself with the many protections of modern science, and has therefore created a degree of security for himself that earlier times did not know. He has achieved this security even though the tradition out of which such security evolved still dictated a contemptuous attitude toward the practical.

But early man nevertheless attended his daily affairs with a certain grudging reverence. Ceremony and ritual were likely to surround such vital functions as hunting and farming, paying homage to the power of the extraordinary to invade and destroy the ordinary. While the measure of security gained thereby was, from the modern rational and scientific point of view, accidental, it nevertheless created for man two overlapping cultural categories, 'the holy and the fortunate, with their opposites, the profane and the unlucky' (Dewey, 1929: 11). These cultural categories were attitudes that characterized dependence and control respectively, and that eventually became distinct realms, the superior of which represented 'occurrences so uncontrollable that they testified to the presence and operations of powers beyond the scope of everyday and mundane things' (Dewey, 1912: 13). That left an 'inferior' realm where a degree of control and prediction was possible, but it was the realm of changing, unstable and profane reality historically denigrated by Plato and Aristotle and the entire tradition of Western philosophy.

> Prosaic beliefs about verifiable facts, beliefs backed up by evidence of the senses and by useful fruits, had little glamour and prestige compared with the vogue of objects of rite and ceremony. (Dewey, 1929: 13)

The point of all this, Dewey argues, is that philosophy (taking its cue from Euclidean geometry) inherits the 'superior realm', the realm previously ruled by religion and regarded as the depository of the sacred and eternal truths, now told not in the language of imagination and myth, but in the language of rational thought and ruled by the canons of formal logic which define the structures of reality such that the illogical is unreal. In fact, the philosophies of Plato and Aristotle are really rational formulations of Greek religion and myth (Dewey, 1929: 16).

So the tradition of Western philosophy that modern man has inherited, Dewey argues, permits the possibility of physical science to the extent that the natural world confirms the dictates of formal logic.

> Thus, along with the elimination of myths and grosser superstitions, there were set up the ideals of science and of a life of reason. Ends which could justify themselves to reason were to take the place of custom as the guide of conduct. These two ideals form a permanent contribution to western civilization. (Dewey, 1929: 16)

But the contribution is an ambivalent one with drastic conditions attached. The two realms which divide reality into the unchanging and eternal truths of philosophy and the changing and temporal conditions of practical activity, mean that, for Western man, the purpose of knowledge is to uncover a pre-existing truth, rather than to bring truth into being through activity in the world. It further means that the operations of the intellect in the purity and security of abstraction have a higher order of priority than the practical activities of men in interaction with their environment, and it also means that there are two different orders of *belief*, one that concerns 'actual existences and the course of events', and the other that concerns ends and values (Dewey, 1929: 18). For Dewey (and for Habermas, as we shall see), the relation between these two modes of belief constitutes one of the major practical problems of our time.

> How shall our most authentic and dependable cognitive beliefs be used to regulate our practical beliefs? How shall the latter serve to organize and integrate our intellectual beliefs? (Dewey, 1929: 18)

The problem was also addressed by Edmund Husserl, the great German phenomenologist, as the crisis of the European sciences: their loss of significance for life (Husserl, 1965). How can the scientist, who lives in a life-world of passions, beliefs, governments, and economies and is subject to all of the claims such interests make on him as a citizen and an individual, maintain his 'objectivity' in the science-world? It was obvious to Husserl, as it was obvious to Dewey (and Habermas) that he cannot, that the questions the scientist asks will shape the answers nature yields.

But, argues Dewey, the Western philosophical tradition will not permit the question, since the two realms (of eternal and unchanging truths on the one hand, and of practical scientific possibilities on the other) are distinct. Moreover, the changing realm of practical activity, precisely because it does change, lacks being, and therefore is less real, and therefore of inferior status and not the proper subject of philosophical consideration. This gives the derogation of the practical a philosophical and ontological justification, and sanctifies the insulation of the practical from both the moral and the purely scientific; for both concern themselves with the immutable, unchanging and eternal truths of internal and external nature as they are defined by a pre-existing and transcendent order. That order, of course, is utterly oblivious to individual human knowing; the act of human knowing, of human investigation and experimentation, does not alter or in any manner affect the pre-existing reality of which it is an imperfect reflection.

The inherited Western tradition involves a number of philosophical conclusions:

(1) The real is rational and the rational is real. There is a complete correspondence between what is cognitively known and what is objectively real.

(2) Only the completely fixed and unchanging can be real, and the completely fixed and unchanging has antecedent existence unaffected by human production and human knowledge.

(3) All special theories of knowledge, whether they be idealist, which hold that the mind and the object known are one, or realist, which reduce knowledge to what exists independently of mind or any variation or combination thereof, all hold

> . . . that what is known is antecedent to the mental act of observation and inquiry, and is totally unaffected by these acts; otherwise it would not be fixed and unchangeable. This negative condition, that the processes of search, investigation, reflection, involved in knowledge relate to something having prior being, fixes once for all the main characters attributed to

mind, and to the organs of knowing. They *must* be outside what is known, so as not to interact in any way with the object to be known . . . . The theory of knowing is modeled after what was supposed to take place in the act of vision. . . . A spectator theory of knowledge is the inevitable outcome. (Dewey, 1929: 23)

Dewey's critique of traditional philosophy and its metaphysics is a critique grounded in the conviction that all thinking is interested thinking, that the quest for certainty that informs traditional epistemologies occludes reality and obstructs attempts to interact with the environment in socially useful ways. Since all knowledge is interested, it is not absolute, and consequently must be of a practical nature, contingent upon the particular intentions of individual actors. The problem with philosophies that attempt to articulate timeless essences, is that what is defined as essential for one philosopher at a given point in time, is inessential from another perspective; in fact, what is defined as essential is merely the particular intention of a particular set of motivations held by particular groups, societies or cultures. That is why we continually re-invent the essential, and can even write histories of human thought according to what each epoch held 'essential' (Hegel, 1956).

Dewey cannot hold to a strict correspondence theory of truth, one in which the truth of an idea depends upon whether it corresponds to an existential referent, because he has abandoned the traditional philosophical distinction between experience of nature and nature itself (Dewey, 1959). Neither can Dewey hold to a strict coherence theory of truth, such as that proposed by idealist philosophy, because if he does, the world disappears, and it is the world that Dewey and all the Progressive philosophers are most concerned to salvage. Dewey is, after all, a social philosopher of the first order, and, insofar as philosophy illuminates the significant problems of man's existential life, it illuminates them in order to solve them, not merely to understand them (although understanding is an important aspect of the solution, as we shall see). Dewey's thought seeks to purge philosophy of such debilitating dualisms as the mind–body problem through an expanded analysis of the operational or behavioral dimensions of such concepts as habits, impulses, and intelligence.

Dewey's analysis of habits is his attempt to bridge, in the behavioral dimension, the traditional philosophical breach between the mind and the bodies or objects of which it has knowledge. In Dewey's analysis, however, the dualisms are recognized in terms of the relationship between an organism and its environment.

> Habits may be profitably compared to physiological functions, like breathing, digesting. The latter are, to be sure, involuntary, while habits are acquired. But important as is this difference for many purposes it should not conceal the fact that habits are like functions in many respects, and especially in requiring the cooperation of organism and environment. Breathing is an affair of the air as truly as of the lungs; digesting an affair of food as truly as of tissues of the stomach. Seeing involves light just as certainly as it does the eye and optic nerve. . . . We may shift from the biological to the mathematical use of the word function, and say that natural operations like breathing and digesting, acquired ones like speech and honesty, are functions of the surroundings as truly as of a person. They are things done *by* the environment by means of organic structures of acquired dispositions. (Dewey, 1922: 14, 15)

Habits are learned; they are either intelligent or routine, and are very much like *arts* in that they involve sensory and motor skills and a degree of finesse. All organisms behave habitually, of course, but the higher organisms have extremely complex and flexible habitual organizations that permit them to function in increasingly complex environments.

Impulses are temporally prior to habits, and are part of man's 'endowment at birth' (Dewey, 1922: 89). They are not specifically organized at inception, but become so only as the organism interacts with its environment, part of which includes other organisms which are acting habitually. Impulses, then, are plastic; they can be adapted to any situation which then bestows upon them meaning within a social context (Dewey, 1922: 95–105).

> In short, the *meaning* of native activities is not native; it is acquired. It depends upon interaction with a matured social

medium. In the case of a tiger or eagle, anger may be identified with a serviceable life-activity, with attack and defense. With a human being it is as meaningless as a gust of wind on a mudpuddle apart from a direction given it by the presence of other persons, apart from the responses they make to it. It is a physical spasm, a blind dispersive burst of wasteful energy. It gets quality, significance, when it becomes a smouldering sullenness, an annoying interruption, a peevish irritation, a murderous revenge, a blazing indignation. (Dewey, 1922: 90)

Intelligence is an acquired habit (Dewey, 1933). Intelligence comes into play in human activity when other more routine habits fail to solve the immediate problem and bring about the desired result. Since man cannot live in a world of his own creation, since man cannot dominate nature with his will, and since man cannot separate himself from his environment through Olympian acts of pure contemplation, man must continually respond, react and readjust to what are often hostile forces in his environment. This requires flexibility and the ability to modify habitual behavior to influence changed circumstances – it requires the ability to *reflect* on one's circumstances and to arrive at a solution to whatever problem has arisen. Reflective thought does not occur without some environmental, social or cultural stimulation, that is, without some penetration of the self by the world of which it is a constituent part. The Aristotelian notion of 'pure thought thinking itself' is fine for the gods, but men need the world to initiate the process and to bring it to fruition. Reflective thought must be an educational aim.

Democracy and Education

In *Democracy and Education: An Introduction to The Philosophy of Education* (1916), Dewey charts the educational course for the Progressive movement and clearly articulates the philosophy of education that gives it credence. He begins with an analysis of that most utilitarian of concepts, *control*, arguing that it is through control of the environment that man continues in existence.

. . . a living being is one that subjugates and controls for its own continued activity the energies that would otherwise use it up. Life is a self-renewing process through action upon the environment. . . . Continuity of life means continual re-adaptation of the environment to the needs of living organisms. (Dewey, 1916: 1, 2)

The continuity of life depends upon, among other things, communication and the transmission of the means of control from generation to generation through the educative process. No generation, much less an individual, could possibly recapitulate the entire history of habits of doing, thinking, and feeling that is the legacy of civilization. Those things exist in the intersubjective understandings of human beings interacting with their environment. The process implies change, transition, adaptation, modification. It implies the perpetuation not only of existing habits of thought, but of the capacity to generate more flexible, subtle habits of thought as the situation elicits them.

From the original impulse to survive, to continue in being, is generated the apparatus of civilizations. That we overlook this less than glamorous origin of human intelligence does not make it any less significant, any less portentous for the human project. Change is the only constant, and change forces man to adapt, to respond to the prerogatives of time and nature. The 'truth' is in the effectiveness of human responses to the changing nature of reality, and those responses are made in a communicative context that infuses them with meaning. The communicative process modifies the posture of all parties to it, and changes the way people perceive the world and respond to it. All communication has this social foundation; for to speak, for Dewey, is to speak *to*, as well as to speak *about*, and, both in the speaking and in the hearing, there is transformation as well as transmission. 'Society not only continues to exist *by* transmission, *by* communication, but it may fairly be said to exist *in* transmission, *in* communication' (Dewey, 1916: 5). Human beings communicate from within the context of a community, which is formed by common understandings, aims, and wisdoms acquired through time by organisms acting in the world. 'Consensus demands communication' (Dewey, 1916: 6).

As societies become increasingly complex, and their interactions with the social and natural environment become correspondingly sophisticated, education in the formal sense of teaching and training, of habituating, becomes increasingly important. This carries with it certain dangers, not the least of which is the creation of a breach between knowledge gained through experience and knowledge acquired through the social and educative process. This is a familiar epistemological problem, made the more real by a highly complex technological society that demands both faith in science and the instrumental power it generates on the one hand, and a healthy respect for independent and creative and often theoretical thought on the other. There must be both education and training, but for Dewey, the veracity of both is grounded in the world, not in some ideal or transcendental conception of essential truth. In this respect he certainly differs from Newman, for whom knowledge was ideal, and for whom the notion that knowledge was power was, to say the least, anathema. The relationship between knowledge and practical life is intimate, Dewey argues (1916: 1), and therefore the educative process must be rooted in the immediate practical and social life of the individual. All knowledge, therefore, has a taint of the practical, of the 'vocational', if for no other reason than its specifically social origins.

> It is the very nature of life to strive to continue in being. Since this continuance can be secured only by constant renewals, life is a self-renewing process. What nutrition and reproduction are to physiological life, education is to social life. This education consists mainly in transmission through communication. (Dewey, 1916: 11)

Education involves the transformation of the quality of experience, bringing it into consonance with the experience of the dominant society in which it takes place. The individual must be led, through the intermediary of the environment, to develop certain propensities for action that fit the aims and purposes of the society that fosters them. The interaction takes place within a natural social environment with which the individual must harmonize. The natural environment consists of 'the things with which a man *varies*' (Dewey, 1916: 13); in the sense of change and evolution, the natural environment consists of the things to which man adapts and addresses his technical expertise. On the other hand, the social environment 'consists of all the activities of fellow beings that are bound up in the carrying on of the activities of any one of its members' (Dewey, 1916: 26). To the extent that the individual becomes part of the *social* activities of his environment, he appropriates the benefits and responsibilities of such interaction. The individual makes them his own, internalizes them, warrants them. In less sanguine times, one might say the individual, through participation or acquiescence in the activities of his social environment, becomes implicated in them, but Dewey is not, at this point, interested in social responsibility as such, merely in developing the ground for education in a democratic society. Nevertheless, he recognizes the implications of socialization for the unreflected consciousness, and states clearly that those habits which lie beneath the level of reflection are those acquired in the course of life in an associated community (Dewey, 1916: 22). The function of the school in such a community is threefold:

(1) To provide a simplified environment for the systematic assimilation of a complex civilization;

(2) To provide a 'purified medium of action', that is, to cull from the history of experience and possibility only those elements consonant with the dominant vision of a 'better future society';

(3) To facilitate the democratic principle of social mobility (Dewey, 1916: 24).

There is fundamental tension between native impulses and the customs and cultures of the social groups of which they are a part. Dewey is aware of the tension, and seeks to ameliorate the authoritarian aspects of social control by insisting on a democratic social order that makes a distinction between control and compulsion. There is no doubt that impulsive activity needs social direction or it might be destructive or wasteful, but direction is accomplished by 'centering the impulses acting at any one time upon some specific end and in introducing an order of continuity into the sequence of acts' (Dewey, 1916: 47). Since every stimulus directs activity, Dewey argues, and since every activity is directed by a stimulus, the stimulus becomes the condition for the realization of the proper function of the organism (Dewey, 1916: 29). Control in this sense is merely the assistance needed to realize what is potential in every organism as it interacts with its social and natural environment. The commonly used philosophical illustration of the point is perception. The organs of sight depend upon the stimulation of light for the realization of their proper function – sight. What sight *means*, the determination of the content of any particular act of vision, is socially conditioned to enable the organism to harmonize itself with its environment. To elevate the analogy to the level of social interaction, Dewey argues that the young accommodate themselves to the action of others in such a manner that their actions become interactions; they have a socially useful content.

> The net outcome of the discussion is that the fundamental means of control is not personal but intellectual. It is not 'moral' in the sense that a person is moved by direct personal appeal from others, important as is this method at critical junctures. It consists in the habits of *understanding*, which are set up in using objects in correspondence with others, whether by way of cooperation and assistance or rivalry and competition. *Mind*, as a concrete thing is precisely the power to understand things in terms of the use made of them; a socialized mind is the power to understand them in terms of the use to which they are turned in joint or shared situations. And mind in this sense is the method of social control. (Dewey, 1916: 39, 40)

This is not to say that there is no such thing as external compulsion; of course there is. But for Dewey compulsion is not the purpose or the method of education. Internal control that brings the individual into consonance with the social environment is accomplished through cultivating a common understanding of the means and ends of social action, and this is the business of education. Democracy is the form of social organization that most efficiently realizes this internalization.

Dewey's notion of democracy involves a realization of the social nature of man, of man's dependence and interdependence upon and with his social environment. In order to be fully human, one must be fully social. Civil privatism, the malaise of the twentieth century, is 'an unnamed form of insanity which is responsible for a large part of the remediable suffering of the world' (Dewey, 1916: 52). The 'rugged individualist' is neither rugged nor solitary, but inextricably involved with others in ways that define his powers. This is obvious, Dewey argues, because we are never concerned with changing the whole environment in which we exist, but only certain specific parts of it – the rest is assumed, taken for granted, and forms the social background against which all our activities take place. The habitual behaviors which are based on this background consensus are rarely subjected to any kind of critique, at least as long as they are instrumentally valid. The active readjustment to specific circumstances in the environment involves another kind of habit, intelligence. Intelligence involves flexibility, plasticity, the ability to change and modify one's relationship to any situation in ways that promote the interests of the organism at any point in time (Dewey, 1933: 100). This kind of active habit is what Dewey means by growth, and growth is the defining characteristic of life itself. It does not have an end, it is the end.

> Habits take the form both of habituation, or a general and persistent balance of organic activities with the surroundings, and of active capacities to readjust activity to meet new conditions. The former furnishes the background of growth; the latter constitute growing. Active habits involve thought, invention, and initiative in applying capacities to new aims. They are opposed to routine which marks an arrest of growth. Since growth is the characteristic of life, education is all one with growing; it has no end beyond itself. (Dewey, 1916: 62)

The educational process has no end beyond itself; it is a constant process of renewal, transformation, reorganization and reconstruction. The purpose of the school as a social institution, is to ensure that the individual continues to grow not only while in the institution, but throughout life. Thus a major purpose of education is to facilitate 'life-long learning'.

The educative activity begins in a blind and impulsive form in that it does not recognize itself in relation to other life activities. Once an impulsive activity becomes enmeshed in the vast array of consequences which attend to it, it takes on meaning and can then become part of an intentional act. This definition of education is instrumental in a different sense than the ordinary. The utility to be derived by education is not merely manipulative control, but growth defined as an end in itself. There is a sense in which whatever promotes the forces of life (growth) is good both morally and practically, and that which destroys or retards life (growth) is detrimental morally and practically. As we shall see, this naïve naturalism distinguishes Dewey's philosophy from the more critical philosophies of the 'post-Holocaust era'.

Dewey establishes the criteria for judging a society, and by implication the educational practice of particular societies, by discussing democracy as the form of social organization most likely to promote the growth of its members. He makes it clear that he wants to avoid setting up an 'ideal' society as the measure because to do so would be to invite charges of impracticality. A good society is one in which there are many interests consciously communicated and shared; and there are varied and free points of contact with other modes of association (Dewey, 1916: 97).

The democratic society he had in mind, of course, is the capitalist society of North America and Europe in the early twentieth century, and that context implies some social relationships that militate against human freedom in the interests of economic efficiency. Dewey does not shy away from these difficult issues, but attempts to address them by arguing that those who sacrifice their lives to mechanical routine must do so for the proper motives (Dewey, 1916: 99). To accept as one's own the purposes and interests of another, without subjecting those purposes and interests to critical analysis (that is, without understanding the socially useful and necessary dimensions of those interests), is the Aristotelian definition of slavery. Technical efficiency may demand the division of labor but it does not logically demand its alienation. Education supplies the means by which society might overcome the alienation of the industrial workplace, and ameliorate the 'distortions of emotional life' that accompany it. Science can illuminate both the methods of efficient operation and the relations of workers to their work and to one another. It is an illegitimate narrowing of science to restrict it to the former only.

Twentieth-century democracies are societies in which communication plays a dominant role. Democracy is not primarily a form of government, but a method of interaction that takes as primary the dignity of the socially constituted individual.

A democracy is more than a form of government; it is primarily a mode of associated living, of conjoint communicated experience. The extension in space of the number of individuals who participate in an interest so that each has to refer his own action to that of others, and to consider the action of others to give point and direction to his own, is equivalent to the breaking down of those barriers of class, race, and national territory which kept men from perceiving the full import of their activity. (Dewey, 1916: 101)

The criteria for measuring the value of a particular form of social organization involve a measure of the extent to which interests are commonly held by all, and of the extent to which various viewpoints and interests can be effectively and freely communicated. The free interaction of all the competing groups in society ensures a varied and vital experience for their members. The more varied the experience, the more intelligence is exercised to account for it and to endow it with meaning. Diversity of opinion is essential to the health and continued growth of any society, but especially of technological societies.

The aim of education, at least in the democratic context, is that which stimulates the capacity for continued growth. Dewey is quite aware of the political implications of educational philosophies which impose social aims on individuals and classes of individuals, thereby robbing them of their essential natures. Since human consciousness is interested, there is always the danger that one interest will predominate to the exclusion of others:

> Wherever social control means subordination of individual activities to class authority, there is danger that industrial education will be dominated by acceptance of the status quo. Differences of economic opportunity then dictate what the future callings of individuals are to be. (Dewey, 1916: 140)

For Dewey, there can be no single aim of education in a democratic society; all particular aims represent the interests of the moment, generally dictated by the imperatives of scarcity and need. The society that best serves the diversity of needs and interests is the society that recognizes the essentially political nature of modern life, and the need for continued associated growth. That society will demand some kind of social return from each of its members, while at the same time providing opportunities for the development of distinctive capacities (Dewey, 1916: 142). Educational aims are rooted in both individual capacities and social need. Social need, in turn, is culturally determined where culture is understood as 'the capacity for constantly expanding the range and accuracy of one's perception of meanings' (Dewey, 1916: 145). Individuals have no meaning apart from their meanings as social beings, and this socially amplified meaning transcends the dictates of mere social efficiency.

Educational aims imply both the interests which focus them, and the disciplines which actuate them. Dewey defines interests as identification with 'the objects which define the activity and which furnish the means and obstacles to its realization' (Dewey, 1916: 161). To have an interest is to recognize the continuity of experience as involving a process with a beginning, a middle, and an end, and to relate the intermediate steps as part of this teleology. This requires 'continuity of attention and endurance', which is what Dewey means by will or discipline (Dewey, 1916: 162). The significance of these descriptions of interest, will, and discipline are ontological and epistemological: ontologically Dewey seeks to implode the dualism between minds that know and bodies that are known by showing that there is no real distinction between thought and action or engagement; epistemologically he seeks to collapse the distinction between the subject matter of learning and its objects by showing that both are infused with meaning by human intentionality.

> The significance of this doctrine for the theory of education is twofold. On the one hand it protects us from the notion that mind and mental states are something complete in themselves, which then happen to be applied to some ready-made objects and topics so that knowledge results. It shows that mind and intelligent or purposeful engagement in a course of action into which things enter are identical. Hence to develop and train mind is to provide an environment which induces such activity. On the other side . . . it shows that subject matter of learning is identical with all objects, ideas, and principles which enter as resources or obstacles into the continuous intentional pursuit of a course of action. (Dewey, 1916: 162)

Human experience is reciprocal: it involves both intentionality, which is the active ingredient in human consciousness, and what

Dewey calls 'undergoing', the passive element (Dewey, 1916: 163). Dewey, like the phenomenologists, for example, Merleau-Ponty, (1962), is concerned with carefully articulating the dynamic and continuous relationship between human consciousness and the world such that neither can exist without the other, and such that neither is primary. When we act in the world, the world in turn acts upon us, and we endure the consequences of our initial action. When we integrate the consequences of our actions into the fabric of our total intentions, it may be said that we are engaged in 'experience' as opposed to mere activity. But experience is not primarily or exclusively cognitive, rather it is reciprocally active and passive. Its meaning, its value, consists in the perception of its interconnectedness with other intentions, experiences and activities. When education focuses exclusively on the acquisitive and cognitive element of experience, it denudes experience of its vitality by making it abstract and passive, by creating the illusion that one can learn *about* experience without being implicated in it. This perpetuates a false ontology and a false epistemology and leads to an anemic pedagogy.

Knowledge cannot be injected into student's minds without introducing them to the intentions that produced it in the first place. The cries of irrelevancy that greeted the classical curriculum in the middle of the nineteenth century and general education in the 1960s were legitimate insofar as the content of the curriculum had come unhooked from the train of intentions that originally informed them. In such an atmosphere knowledge becomes something that is acquired, something quite apart from 'thinking', something passive and utterly forgettable. This should come as no surprise, Dewey argues, when the nature of human thought is reckoned.

> Thought, or reflection . . . is the discernment of the relation between what we try to do and what happens in consequence. No experience having a meaning is possible without some element of thought. . . . Thinking is thus equivalent to an explicit rendering of the intelligent element in our experience. It makes it possible to act with an end in view. It is the condition of our having aims. (Dewey, 1916: 169–71)

The mere registering of information, its acquisition and storage,

,s not thinking. The illusion that this activity is thinking, is pervasive and pernicious. All genuine thinking involves the relationship between what is and what might or ought to be at some time in the future; all thinking is interested, intentional.

Thinking occurs when things are not as they should be, when things are 'going on' that are perplexing and require intentional action for their resolution. Problematic situations elicit thoughtful inquiry that usually takes the following form:

(1) formulation of a preliminary interpretation of the situation, a preliminary hypothesis;

(2) investigation of the problem with a view to a solution;

(3) the formulation of a formal hypothesis; and

(4) the testing of the hypothesis, which involves commitment and action (Dewey, 1916: 176).

For Dewey, all thought is original research, and ought to be encouraged by educational institutions charged with the preparation of students for life in an uncertain world (Dewey, 1916: 174, 178).

The essential educative experience must be rooted in the students' life processes such that it has immediate and continuing meaning for them, that is, it must be a real problem that develops within the students' frame of intentions. The problem then stimulates thought in conformity with the processes enumerated above, provided the students have the proper attitudes of straightforwardness, flexibility, integrity of purpose and open-mindedness requisite to the task. Such thought, since it is not isolated from action, also requires a willingness to accept the social consequences that issue from it and give it its essential meaning (Dewey, 1916: 193–226).

The abstractions of academics are to some extent justified by the extraordinarily complex and varied nature of human experience, which experience cannot be had in its fulness by any single individual. If principles of value are taught directly to the young, unmediated by experience, there is the risk that students will learn to parrot the values thus imparted while secretly harboring different, often contradictory, sets of values by which they conduct themselves. This is often done unconsciously, and it creates a habit of mind that is at home with valuational and aesthetic contradiction. For example, students might learn publicly to espouse the virtues of Christian morality while privately acting in accordance with some other, less altruistic code of conduct; or might learn publicly to 'appreciate' Mozart while privately preferring some other form of musical expression more closely representative of their experience. Nevertheless, it is necessary to represent experiences distant from the immediate in order to ensure a sense of continuity, of history, of the diversity and openness of human civilization and experience. The real danger is that the representation of experience can become a substitute for experience itself, resulting in an academic 'bookishness' that is contrary to the true nature of experience. Such an attitude facilitates a breach between theory and practice.

The relative value of any particular course of study, an academic discipline, is fixed by the situation into which it enters. This situational ethic in regard to the valuation of academic disciplines means that, apart from some specific social context in which a choice must be made, all subjects are to be valued equally. This does not, for Dewey, mean that there is a general devaluation of all courses of study, because there is no consciousness at all apart from a situation in which choices must be made; he is simply arguing that 'Insofar as any study has a unique or irreplaceable function in experience, insofar as it marks a characteristic enrichment of life, its worth is intrinsic or incomparable' (Dewey, 1916: 281). So it makes no sense to value the intrinsic over the instrumental (or vice versa), since all contribute to the total human experience, and since all will be valued according to the dictates of a specific social situation.

> The tendency to assign separate values to each study and to regard the curriculum in its entirety as a kind of composite made by the aggregation of segregated values is a result of the isolation of social groups and classes. Hence it is the business of education in a democratic social group to struggle against this isolation in order that the various interests may reinforce and play into one another. (Dewey, 1916: 292)

The divisions of labor in the industrial economy are represented in education as the divisions of academic labor and training. The isolation attendant on economic divisions of labor is paralleled in the educational system and imported into academic life at all levels. The problem for a theory of educational valuation is to reconcile these competing and diverse interests into an integral unity that illuminates and enriches experience in a democratic society (Dewey, 1916: 219), without destroying the diversity that makes life interesting and growth possible. The original social division that gave rise to a supporting educational philosophy was the social division in Greek society between freeman and slave, which fostered the educational distinction between culture and utility. This distinction, while pervasive, is neither absolute nor necessary. The necessity to labor for material subsistence is part of the human condition, but the existence of a slave class that concerned itself exclusively with this function and facilitated a leisured class with the material and temporal capital necessary to create (and consume) culture is an historical phenomenon. In Greek society this social division was legitimated by an epistemology that divided human activity into the lower, menial and utilitarian realms, and the higher, intellectual and rational realms. Social classes legitimized themselves by an appeal to human nature, which presumably was immutable, and which divided humanity on the one hand into those for whom rational thought was possible, and for whom self-determination was desirable, and on the other those ruled by the passions, for whom self-determination was neither desirable nor possible. To the extent that Western society has perpetuated these divisions it has remained a class society, and to that extent is not democratic.

If the opportunities for both productive labor and cultivated leisure were equally distributed within and throughout a society, there would be no conflict between doing and knowing, between practice and theory, between desire and reason (Dewey, 1916: 293). Educational theory would then be concerned with maximizing the interrelations of each for the benefit of all.

> Only when a division of these interests coincides with a division of an inferior and a superior social class will preparation for useful work be looked down upon with contempt as an unworthy thing: a fact which prepares one for the conclusion that the rigid identification of work with material interests, and leisure with ideal interests is itself a social product. (Dewey, 1916: 294)

The problem for education in a democratic society is to abolish the dualism, both epistemologically and politically, and to allocate social capital in ways that facilitate free communication among all 'classes', and interests in the society (Dewey, 1916 292).

Dewey is concerned to demonstrate his opposition to philosophical dualisms by showing that they are essentially aristocratic and anti-democratic, and that they unwittingly perpetuate a class antagonism that is utterly hostile to the kind of democracy to which the progressive movement was committed. The supremacy of reason over the passions, in the thought of Plato and Aristotle, has been imported into modern consciousness as a contempt for both experience as a form of doing and for experience as interested. The first form the prejudice takes is the predisposition for logical coherence, the second, the penchant for disinterested observation. But, on the one hand Dewey argues that logical coherence has no meaning apart from its engagement in the world, and on the other that perception is not passive and disinterested but active and intentional. The business of the school, therefore, is not to inoculate students with the knowledge of the past as if that were enough to ensure proper action in the future, but to enable the students to select activities from their past and from their cultural inheritance, as well as from their present environment, that will inform their future intentions as social intentions, and as intentions consonant with the dictates of life in a truly democratic society. In other words, scientific 'progress' cannot be considered apart from *doing*, that is, apart from action in the world; and action in the world implies social and political consequences that must be part of the initial intention (Dewey, 1916: 321).

The individual is isolated and autonomous in neither the epistemological nor in the political sense. A society that is legitimated by custom and tradition will encourage its members to define the limits of their individuality within the limits of behavior and thought prescribed by the extant culture, and such a society will place a premium on uniformity and stability, whether or not that society makes a claim to being democratic. A *progressive* society, on the other hand, has a direct interest in promoting a variety of perspectives and intentions among its members, since this variety is what makes the social experience fertile enough to promote growth. If education is an end in itself when it promotes growth, and if experience requires diversity as a condition for the development of intelligent behavior, then a

democratic society which encourages and facilitates the individual differences of its members, and an educational system
which encourages both preservation and diversification of cultural products, are symbiotic. Since the educational process is
never neutral, democratic societies seek their own preservation
as educational societies in which growth is the ultimate value.

The theory of the method of knowing which is advanced . . .
may be termed pragmatic. Its essential feature is to maintain
the continuity of knowing with an activity which purposely
modifies the environment . . . since democracy stands in principle for free interchange, for social continuity, it must develop
a theory of knowledge which sees in knowledge the method by
which one experience is made available in giving direction
and meaning to another. The recent advances in physiology,
biology, and the logic of the experimental sciences supply the
specific intellectual instrumentalities demanded to work out
and formulate such a theory. Their educational equivalent is
the connection of the acquisition of knowledge in the schools
with activities, or occupations, carried on in a medium of
associated life. (Dewey, 1916: 400–1)

Dewey's philosophy is everywhere concerned with the destruction of the dualisms that have plagued Western thought. Nowhere is this more evident than in his theory of morality for the
democratic society. Where epistemological dualisms become
ethical dualisms, and sanction the diremption of motives and
deeds, interests and principles, the separation between thought
and action results in a political environment where critical
thought is never translated into action; where the status quo is
legitimated by epistemological considerations. The retreat is to a
realm of pure thought, pure reason, and the result is a narrow
morality with which ordinary knowledge and everyday thought
has nothing to do, in which 'conscience is thought of as
something radically different from consciousness' (Dewey, 1916:
411).

But morals are not so narrowly conceived; rather, they
embrace all of our relationships with others, the intentions which
inform them and the consequences which issue from them. We
are accustomed to speaking about morals with reference to
specific virtues (such as honesty, loyalty, courage), but morals

really concern all of our interrelationships with our social and
natural environments.

> Morals concern nothing less than the whole character, and the
> whole character is identical with the man in all his concrete
> make-up and manifestations. To possess virtue does not
> signify to have cultivated a few nameable and exclusive traits;
> it means to be fully and adequately what one is capable of
> becoming through association with others in all the offices of
> life. (Dewey, 1916: 415)

Social interactions and-intentions frame the parameters of what
is morally acceptable at any given time. Moral education reflects
these social intentions in their historical and ecological complexity. In order to do this effectively, the educational institution
must be an adequate reflection of the social environment insofar
as it embodies the principles of democratically associated living,
and it must connect with the large social milieu of which it is an
integral part. Schools, and by implication universities, must
promote the growth of their members and the enlargement of
their experience in a communal context characterized by openness to the variety of perceptions of the past and intentions for
the future, for to be conscious is continually to begin afresh
(Dewey, 1916: 417). In this sense education is thoroughly moral.

Principles and Assumptions of Dewey's Progressivism

– The dualisms that have plagued Western philosophy are
rooted in a quest for certainty which is a result of the material
insecurity seen as the existential fate of man. The apparatus of
civilizations is generated from the original impulse to survive.
– In its quest for certainty, Western culture has derogated the
practical and apotheosized the theoretical, resulting in problematic epistemologies, ontologies, and ethics.
– The major philosophical problem for modern man is the
relationship between the instrumental and the moral; between
science and ethics.
– All thinking is interested thinking. The quest for certainty
that informs traditional epistemologies occludes the reality of
experience, its reciprocal and historical nature.

– Truth is neither a matter of the correspondence of thoughts with their objects, nor is it a matter of coherence of thoughts with themselves, but rather a matter of the correspondence of interests with the consequences of behavior.

– Intelligence is an acquired habit; reflective thought an educational aim.

– The continuity of civilized life depends upon the effective communication of proven techniques for survival. Society, for better or worse, exists in this communication and transmission.

– The relation between knowledge and practical life is both reciprocal and intimate.

– Education involves the transformation of the quality of experience, through the interactions of individuals with their natural and social environments.

– The educational process has no end beyond itself; it is a constant process of renewal, transformation, reorganization and reconstruction. The purpose of the school (and the university) is to ensure growth.

– Democracy is the form of political organization most likely to promote the growth of its members, since it encourages the conscious communication of a variety of perspectives and intentions, and it facilitates free contact with other modes of associated life.

– Individuals have no meaning apart from their meaning as social beings. Civil privatism is a modern form of insanity.

– The essential educative experience must connect to the students' life such that it has immediate and continuing meaning for them.

– The relative value of any particular course of study is fixed by the situation into which it enters. Apart from the situation, all courses are to be valued equally.

– Education which develops the capacities for associated living is by definition moral.

ESSENTIALISM

Historical Background

Of the four approaches to general education, Essentialism is perhaps the most familiar, the most celebrated and the most misunderstood. Its major proponent and author is the mercurial Robert Maynard Hutchins, who argued passionately for the Great Books program at the University of Chicago in the 1930s and 1940s while he was president of that institution. Hutchins' concern was the apparent dilution of the American undergraduate curriculum by the advocates of professionalism and vocationalism who had gained control of the curriculum since the end of the First World War. He saw the curricula of higher education as confused, without any particular unifying principles, and adrift in a sea of consumerism and anti-intellectualism. His somewhat vituperative language was directed at those for whom the traditional liberal education had become irrelevant to contemporary life, and for whom education meant training for employment in a modern technological state. His criticism was at times strident, at times even hysterical, but it was justified by the rise of world fascism and the clear danger that the institutions of democratic society were threatened not only from without by militarism and totalitarianism, but also from within by apathy and greed (Hutchins, 1947: 39).

Essentialism is similar to Idealism in that it recognizes cultural diversity insofar as diverse cultures might have general education programs that differ substantially from one another in their specific content. Essentialist general education is not a survey of the common learning of all cultures, but an intensive immersion in the essential expressions of one of them – in our case, Western civilization. Idealism, on the other hand, is much broader, more inclusive, and addresses all cultures in their ideal nature as having the same truths (that are pre-existent rather than emergent) that exist in all cultures and at all times in recognizable and ideal forms. Idealism is historically prior to Essentialism, and is the product of a much less cosmopolitan culture. Essentialism is, to that extent at least, a modern expression of Idealist sentiment; it was born in the age of total war and emerged as a counterweight to fascism.

Essentialists claim to know what is essential, whereas Idealists claim only that there is an ideal truth that expresses itself differently in various cultures and at different times, but is nevertheless eternal and unchanging. Essentialists may be idealists, but they are idealists of a more culturally diverse and epistemologically unsettled world – a world where the consequences of moral relativism are much more immediately evident than the consequences of an intellectual authoritarianism. If from the perspective of 40 years his writings seem curiously authoritarian, it is well to remember that Hutchins was writing in the shadow of European Fascism, and largely in response to what he perceived to be the malaise of American democracy: materialism and intellectual apathy.

Hutchins' Lament

Hutchins saw higher learning in America beset by three dilemmas: professionalism and vocationalism; isolationism; and anti-intellectualism. These dilemmas were, in turn, the unfortunate side-effects of a commodity culture in which the love of money was the chief motivating factor (Hutchins, 1936). The lack of financial resources for higher education put the institutions of higher learning in the position of having to market themselves, of having to enter into compromising relationships with business and government, and of training its students for specific, narrow and often vocational careers. This dependence on public support produced institutions entirely too willing to compromise their standards, their missions, and their students' welfare to the demands of a short-sighted market economy. The result is the 'service station' concept of the university in which every conceivable manifestation of the public interest becomes legitimized by course offerings and degrees and suitable academic credentialing (Hutchins, 1936: 5, 6). For Hutchins there was no longer any coherence, no unifying purpose to American higher education other than that which was supplied by a whimsical and apparently unstable economy (Hutchins, 1947: 40).

A confused notion of democracy and the role of higher education in a democratic society further complicates the issue. Hutchins argued that democracy had been illegitimately used to justify an unproductive and ultimately undemocratic relationship between institutions of higher education and the society which they were supposed to serve. If anyone can be admitted to any course of study at any time for any reason, the quality of higher education suffers. The notion that a democratic society demands equal educational opportunity for everyone, regardless of ability, preparation, or motivation, is based on the mistaken assumption that higher education exists primarily to provide access to the vast system of economic rewards that a democratic and capitalist society provides (Hutchins, 1936: 14). That is not the case. In fact, Hutchins argues, the contrary is the case: the university can make its contribution to a democratic society only if it is allowed to become the home of independent intellectual work, and that means intellectual work that is not solely the expression of instrumental intentions. The curriculum that must be open to everyone is the general education curriculum, the curriculum he proposes to replace the last two years of high school and the first two years of college, and that ends with the BA degree. The content of this general education is not immediately evident, Hutchins argues, because we have lost the notion of a common cultural heritage that is the basis for all that follows. We have lost it, because we have become immersed in the pursuit of the trivial.

The general education curriculum also serves the function of protecting the university from the colleges and vice versa; a university that attempts to do college work either does a poor job of being a university or a poor job of being a college, but it cannot do a good job of both (Hutchins, 1936: 8, 9). This is because in order to stimulate enrollments, a university must attract students, and in order to attract students it must offer courses, programs and services that lead to the kinds of lives that society has come to expect for its young. To the degree that an institution fulfills these expectations, it attracts students, but these functions are not the functions that an essential general education addresses. General education, Hutchins argues, is not a marketable educational commodity.

All that is wrong with American higher education centers on an erroneous notion of progress. If progress is defined in material terms, if it is defined quantitatively as the acquisition of more information, more technological expertise, more control over the environment, then it stands to reason that the general education that Hutchins deems essential is really irrelevant. It is concerned with quality in a world gone crazy with quantity.

> Our notion of progress is that everything is getting better and must be getting better from age to age. Our information is increasing. Our scientific knowledge is expanding. Our technological equipment in its range and excellence is far superior to what our fathers or even our older brothers knew. . . . In intellectual fields, therefore, we have no hesitancy in breaking

completely with the past; the ancients did not know the things we know; they had never seen steam engines, or aeroplanes, or radios, and seem to have had little appreciation of the possibilities of the factory system. Since these are among the central facts in our lives, how can the ancients have anything to do with us? . . . We begin, then, with a notion of progress and end with an anti-intellectualism which denies, in effect, that man is a rational animal . . . the idea that his education should consist of the cultivation of his intellect is, of course, ridiculous. What it must consist of is surveys, more or less detailed, of the modern industrial, technological, financial, political and social situation so that he can fit himself into it with a minimum of discomfort to himself and to his fellow men. Thus the modern temper produces that strangest of modern phenomena, an anti-intellectual university (Hutchins, 1936: 24–7).

The problem is much more serious than it first appears, because Hutchins is convinced that the health of the nation, the vitality of democracy itself, is dependent on the integrity of higher education, while the integrity of higher education is in its turn dependent on the health of the democratic society that gives it life. The two institutions are mutually dependent, and serve one another's most essential interests. But for Hutchins, it is the university and the college that must overcome the circularity of dependency and devote themselves to the advancement of knowledge, and to the cultivation of the intellectual virtues.

This is not to be an easy task, Hutchins fears, largely because of the fragmentation of the curriculum caused by a professionalism that degenerates into vocationalism and encourages an intellectual territoriality that inhibits communication across disciplinary lines and encourages anti-intellectualism in American academic life. The university has been too quick to respond to the needs and whims of the society it mirrors, and consequently it can no longer authenticate the content of the professional curricula. Hutchins fears that this trend will expand, and infect all of the academic disciplines, for nearly all of them are associated with some sort of professional training. Yet each of the professions has a rich intellectual heritage that ought to be the focus of its curriculum. The progressive spirit, in its more excessive expressions, has denigrated this heritage in favor of a

more 'practical' professional education that is more immediately
tied to the current needs of society. This, Hutchins argues, is
lamentable. If each of the learned professions were to recapture
its intellectual heritage, and focus on it as the essential object of
its inquiry, many of the confusions surrounding the university
curriculum could be overcome.

> . . . the unifying principle of a university is the pursuit of truth
> for its own sake. So far as professional departments adopt this
> principle as their own they take their place in the university's
> community of scholars. If the number of professional groups
> can be limited to those that have intellectual content; if they
> and all other departments can conduct their work in the same
> spirit; if we can develop general education so that all ad-
> vanced study will rest on a common body of knowledge, we
> may succeed in making our universities true communities of
> true scholars. (Hutchins, 1936: 57)

Hutchins was acutely aware of the consequences of anti-
intellectualism in democratic societies. He watched with horror
as the Fascists wiped clean the moral horizons of Europe, and
implicated the universities in their efforts. Hutchins had an
'abiding faith in the highest powers of mankind' and wanted
them held constantly before the American public during these
dark and dangerous years.

General Education: The Great Books Program

Hutchins saw the need for a common ground from which
intellectual dialogue on the pressing issues of modern civilization
might emerge; without a common ground, specialists in the
university could never talk to one another, and their students
were doomed to the same social and intellectual alienation.

> Unless students and professors (and particularly professors)
> have a common intellectual training, a university must remain
> a series of disparate schools and departments, united by
> nothing except the fact that they have the same president and
> board of trustees. Professors cannot talk to one another, not at
> least about anything important. They cannot hope to under-
> stand one another. (Hutchins, 1936: 59)

The danger in this situation is one Hutchins does not directly address. The common assumption working in an educational system that has no general education component is that there is no need to discuss the traditions that hold us together because they are clear and obvious. The rise of Fascism showed the world how dangerous this attitude can be.

The general education system Hutchins envisioned was based on the Great Books of Western civilization, and involved the study of these common texts between the junior year of high school and the sophomore year of college. Everyone who could learn from books was to have this education, without exception. For most, the end of the sophomore year would mark the end of their formal education and would be signified by the BA degree. Higher education would be limited to those with the ability to do what amounted to graduate-level work in the university. Those who could not learn from books raised special pedagogical problems, but they were to be included in the educational experience and resources were to be dedicated to solving their special difficulties.

At the heart of Hutchins' notion of general education was his conviction that general education ought to be for everyone, regardless of whether they go on to higher education, and regardless of any particular practical value it might have. It involves the training and cultivation of the 'intellectual virtues', by which Hutchins means the Aristotelian virtues as refined and systematized by Thomas Aquinas. These intellectual powers are to be trained and disciplined in order that the intellect might be properly habituated to work well in any field (Hutchins, 1936: 63). This is hardly a new insight in the history of American higher education; the same arguments were made for the preservation of a different curriculum by the authors of the *Yale Report* of 1828 (Hofstadter and Smith (eds), 1961: 275–91). The notion that properly trained intellectual virtues are equally applicable to any intellectual endeavor was not a notion hospitable to prevailing practices of progressivist education, however. The focus of education in the 1930s was on the immediate, the practical, and the instrumental. The critical appreciation of cultural artifacts in the form of careful perusal of the 'Great Books' was a notion popular only at the University of Chicago, and there only under the auspices of Hutchins' strong personality. In fact, many authors argued against Hutchins' prescriptions because they saw them as authoritarian and to some extent arbitrary (Gideonse, 1937: 6–10).

A strange and erroneous notion of progress was responsible for the death of the liberal arts and the subsequent fragmented and trivial college curricula. Scientific progress had as its price the division of scientific labor, the specialization of scientific and technological disciplines, and the extension of the scientific method into all spheres of human intellectual activity. It also meant a society in which change was more evident than stability, and where old traditions and truths were seen as fetters on the development of scientific possibilities. In such an environment it is no wonder that educational authorities saw the need to educate for a changing world, and to prepare students to live in such a world by making them adaptable. But, as Hutchins points out, adaptability is not without political and moral consequences, and one function of education addresses these consequences.

> One purpose of education is to draw out the elements of our common human nature. These elements are the same in any time or place. The notion of educating a man to live in any particular time or place, to adjust him to any particular environment, is therefore foreign to a true conception of education.
>
> Education implies teaching. Teaching implies knowledge. Knowledge is truth. Truth is everywhere the same. Hence education should be everywhere the same. I do not overlook the possibilities of differences in organization, in administration, in local habits and customs. These are details. I suggest that the heart of any course of study designed for the whole people will be, if education is rightly understood, the same at any time, in any place, under any political, social, or economic conditions. (Hutchins, 1936: 66)

When education is rightly understood, it is the cultivation of the intellect according to the metaphysical principles of Aristotle and Aquinas in order to ensure 'correct thinking' (Hutchins, 1936: 67).

But it is characteristic of the time, Hutchins argues, to ask the schools to do things that other social institutions are better prepared and positioned to do. Public school educators sometimes act as though no other social institutions have an educative function, and in doing so coax from their proper context social processes that would better remain in churches, families, cities, newspapers, movies, or other social institutions. It is not necessary to make an academic discipline out of all social phenomena; on the contrary,

> . . . [I]t is a good principle of educational administration that a college or university should do nothing that another agency can do as well . . . (Hutchins, 1936: 70)

That means that general education, rather than substituting for some other social institution in preparing the student for life, should be restricted to its proper function: intellectual training, regardless of whether the students think such training is valuable or relevant.

The consent of general education is not subject to the preferences of faculty or students, it is dictated by the necessities of history and good judgment, and it inheres in our intellectual traditions as those traditions are revealed to us through the Great Books. Hutchins was utterly opposed to the educational practice that allowed undergraduates to choose their courses and plan their education with no organizing principle in mind other than their personal preferences.

> The free elective system as Mr. Eliot introduced it at Harvard and as Progressive Education adapted it to lower levels amounted to a denial that there was content to education. Since there was no content to education, we might as well let students follow their own bent. . . . This overlooks the fact that the aim of education is to connect man with man, to connect the present with the past, and to advance the thinking of the race. If this is the aim of education, it cannot be left to the sporadic, spontaneous interests of children or even of undergraduates. (Hutchins, 1936: 71)

General education is concerned with what human beings have in common, with what can be referred to as our species-being, rather than with what makes each of us, within a given cultural context, individuals (individual-being). Those matters relevant to our particular situation are, or at least may be, irrelevant to our situation as members of the species, as extensions of the cultural traditions of the West. Such matters as technology, current events, body and character building are excluded from the general education curricula, not because they are unimportant to us as individuals, but because they are irrelevant to the task of articulating our common nature (Hutchins, 1936: 74, 75).

General education can be had only by examining the original texts, by struggling through what great thinkers of Western culture have thought about the human condition. Hutchins distrusts textbooks because they dilute the content of the classics in their misguided attempt to make them 'accessible'. The content of general education must be kept pure, because the course of study thus established is the repository of our inheritance.

> We have then for general education a course of study consisting of the greatest books of the western world and the arts of reading, writing, thinking, and speaking, together with mathematics, the best exemplar of the processes of human reason. If our hope has been to frame a curriculum which educes the elements of our common human nature, this program should realize our hope. If we wish to prepare the young for intelligent action, this course of study should assist us; for they will have learned what has been done in the past, and what the greatest men have thought. They will have learned how to think themselves. If we wish to lay a basis for advanced study, that basis is provided. If we wish to secure true universities, we may look forward to them, because students and professors may acquire through this course of study a common stock of ideas and common methods of dealing with them. (Hutchins, 1936: 85)

Beyond General Education: The Higher Learning

The higher learning takes place after the sophomore year of college, and includes the upper division undergraduate, graduate, and professional curricula. Hutchins considers the university's primary function teaching (that is, it is an educational institution); he considers the research function ancillary and of

scientific inquiry becomes possible in the first place (Hutchins, 1947: 22–6). To deny the fundamental human interests in wisdom, goodness, and the good life, is to make a metaphysical argument. To assume a posture of neutrality, of objectivity, of detachment toward nature and toward other human beings as components of nature is to assume a metaphysical position which has as its ultimate value the control and mastery of nature. And that is the contemporary predicament. Society is efficient but not 'good', even though it is good to be efficient. This definition of good, in Hutchins' view, was a materialist conception that had devastating consequences for modern man.

> The notion that a just and equitable distribution of goods will be achieved by the advance of technology or that by its aid we shall put material goods in their proper relation to all others is reduced to absurdity by the coincidence of the zenith of technology and the nadir of moral and political life. (Hutchins, 1947: 40)

Metaphysics is what holds the world together, its denigration is the denigration of the world. In 1947, the recent experiences of economic depression, moral decay and world war so fresh in memory told Hutchins that much. His prescription for a healthy society may have sounded extreme and authoritarian to some of his contemporaries (Gideonse, 1937), but his prescription for a healthy university, and its relation to a democratic society have been taken seriously by advocates of general education ever since.

For Hutchins the standards by which the modern university ought to be judged were set by the extent to which it clearly and critically addressed the central issues of the day. Whenever societies lose their common cultural ideals, they lose the ability to ground critical thought on anything but expediency and instrumentalism (Hutchins, 1947: 105). The followers of John Dewey, the so called 'progressives', had lost the common ground, had abdicated it in favor of a facile pedagogical instrumentalism and moral situationalism in which moral commitment and cultural vision were impossible. John Dewey would never have condoned such thoroughgoing materialism, and would not have recognized his own philosophy in it.

Principles and Assumptions of Hutchins' Essentialism

– There is an objective standard for truth, goodness, and right and those standards are discoverable by man through the use of his reason, even though they may not be objectively or scientifically verifiable (Hutchins, 1947: 86).

– The end of man is the full development of his intellectual powers (Hutchins, 1947: 87).

– Man's full intellectual powers may best be developed, and the freedom of his mind best guaranteed by a discipline which forms habits that enable the mind to operate well (Hutchins, 1947: 91).

– Education, rightly understood, is the cultivation of the intellect according to the metaphysical principles of Aristotle and Aquinas, which will ensure right thinking (Hutchins, 1936: 67).

– Democracy is the best form of political organization to ensure that the ends of man can be pursued by all (Hutchins, 1947: 93).

– Universities should be judged by the extent to which they engage in critical thinking about the fundamental issues of our time (Hutchins, 1947: 101), their unifying principle is the pursuit of truth for its own sake.

– General education is for everyone, regardless of any particular instrumental value it might have, and regardless of the student's intellectual ability. Special methods of delivery may need to be developed for those who cannot learn from the Great Books.

PRAGMATISM

Historical Background

Clark Kerr's revised version of *The Uses of the University* (1982), is a response to the changed circumstances of American higher education in the post-Second World War era, an era marked by increasing involvement by the federal government in higher education through grants for research into problems related to defense, scientific and technical progress and health (Kerr, 1982:

54). This federal involvement created an educational environment unlike anything the world has seen, an environment in
which huge quantities of resources are expended to meet a
totally new array of possibilities of which the university never
before conceived. Kerr's is a descriptive study, at least in its
thrust, and not a prescription for, nor necessarily an endorse-
ment of, the status quo. In the 'Postscript – 1972' Kerr laments
the misunderstandings provoked by the book immediately after
its publication in 1963, but takes his detractors to task for
misinterpreting, and misrepresenting his intentions:

> Yet some people have taken analysis to be approval and
> description to be defense, and to assume or to claim that every
> act of every multiversity was both approved and defended in
> these lectures. Thus I learned how easily some persons who
> call themselves scholars can turn a descriptive 'is' into a
> prescriptive 'should be' and then attack the false 'should be'.
> (Kerr, 1982: 147)

We may take it, then, that Kerr's analysis is primarily descriptive, but descriptive of a reality that calls forth different responses from those in the reality that gave rise to Newman's
Idealism, Dewey's Progressivism and certainly Hutchins'
Essentialism. If there is prescription in Kerr's description, it is in
what he chooses to describe, and the manner in which he
describes it. The description reveals a social and cultural
environment qualitatively different from the prewar environment of Hutchins et al. His description implies a political and
moral flexibility that Hutchins, for one, would find anemic, and
an adaptability that Dewey would find ambiguous at best.
Newman's Idealism, Kerr frequently points out, is utterly
incompatible with the educational milieu of the mid-twentieth
century. Perhaps he is right, but occasionally his analysis goes
beyond description, despite his protestations.

Nevertheless, Kerr's book attempts to redefine the contemporary American university in a way that sets it apart from other
universities, and from its own history. His analysis takes into
account such important educational watersheds as the land
grant movement and the federal incursions into educational
policy, and describes the resulting pluralism of the modern
research university, which he dubs the 'multiversity'.

The multiversity is an inconsistent institution. It is not one community but several – the community of the undergraduate and the community of the scientist; the communities of the professional schools; the community of all the nonacademic personnel; the community of the administrators . . . . A community, like the medieval communities of masters and students, should have common interests; in the multiversity, they are quite varied, even conflicting. A community should have a soul, a single animating principle; and the multiversity has several – some of them quite good, although there is much debate on which souls really deserve salvation. (Kerr, 1982: 18, 19)

Kerr means by the term 'multiversity' an institution no longer animated by one ideal or essential notion or body of notions, but rather, a pluralistic institution that has several purposes, several centers of power, clienteles, communities and gods. It is an institution which reflects the society that sponsors it, a society so pluralistic that no single, unifying body of knowledge can adequately reflect its diversity, nor satisfy its constituents (Kerr, 1982; 136, 137). The multiversity is the research university in all its complexity, in all its bewildering contradictions, in all its conflicting and interested politics. It has no absolute center, and there is no single principle that motivates its many players. In fact, it is characterized more by conflict than consensus, though consensus is what its effective leaders pursue (Kerr, 1982: 129), more by flux and dynamic change than by the eternal truths of a less complex day, more by contiguity than coherence.

In short, the multiversity is not analogous to the village community with its priests, but to the modern city in all its infinite variety (Kerr, 1982: 41). The analogy is appropriate, it would seem, at least in the sense that individuals find themselves within one of the many 'subcultures' of the large research institution, rather than within some central organ of the whole. The multiversity is too large to be comprehended in its entirety, too various to stifle individual creativity, no matter how eccentric:

As against the village and the town, the 'city' is more like the totality of civilization as it has evolved and more an integral part of it; and movement to and from the surrounding society has been greatly accelerated. As in a city, there are many separate endeavors under a single rule of law. (Kerr, 1982: 41)

What constitutes this single rule of law? Kerr is unclear on the point, but he seems to mean the administrative organization of campus life; such matters as parking and housing, rather than any organic conception of the law. He may also mean the law of the academic market place, where students choose the courses and services they want and need, and thereby determine the curricular direction of the institution in ways that directly mirror economic choices in the American society.

The Fall From Unity

The university started as a single community – a community of masters and students. It may even be said to have had a soul in the sense of a central animating principle. (Kerr, 1982: 1)

The original unity described and advocated by Cardinal Newman has been lost, according to Kerr, largely as a consequence of the loss of the same unity in the larger society that sustains the university. The original university, by which Kerr means the medieval university, was indeed a community of scholars and students with a commonly held body of assumptions about the nature of the world and about the value of their educational endeavors, assumptions often held in the face of indifference and hostility from the uninitiated who lived their lives outside the academic cloister. Newman abhorred the utilitarian and instrumental attitudes that were becoming current even in his own day, and saw philosophy as the end of the university; the connected view of the world that comes from the exercise of thought or reason upon knowledge. This attitude apotheosized the English model of Oxford, where teaching in an intellectual community was the proper end of the university, good for its own sake regardless of any benefits that might redound to the society.

But even as Cardinal Newman wrote, the German universities were becoming the model for educational and scientific innovation in the United States. The emphasis on graduate research became the hallmark of Johns Hopkins University under Daniel

Coit Gilman, and by the end of the nineteenth century, graduate schools and graduate education had.come to America with a vengeance.

By 1852, when Newman wrote, the German universities were becoming the new model. The democratic and industrial and scientific revolutions were all well underway in the western world. The gentleman 'at home in any society' was soon to be at home in none. Science was beginning to take the place of moral philosophy, research the place of teaching. (Kerr, 1982: 3, 4).

Kerr's historical description of the development of the American university in the nineteenth century conforms to historical convention. The English college gave to the American institutions the model for undergraduate teaching, while the German universities gave them the model for graduate research. The problem arose when the former was neglected in order that the latter might flourish. The emphasis on graduate research, particularly among undergraduate faculty, marked the rise of instrumental reason in the flow of events that eventually resulted in the advent of the multiversity. The new research-oriented university was obliged to associate with new constituencies in order to find necessary financial and political sustenance. This research led to objections by those who deplored the resulting 'service station' concept of the university (a term coined by Abraham Flexner), as being a vulgar and cheapened version of what the true university was all about (Kerr, 1982: 4–6).

The fragmentation of knowledge in the modern world was caused by a combination of factors, as Kerr acknowledges, but its instantiation in the American university can be traced to two: the industrial revolution that gave birth to the German model, and the land grant movement that gave birth to the uniquely American notion of service. The three functions of the modern university – teaching, research and service – were well established by 1930, according to Kerr, and the resulting confusion concerning the true nature of higher education in America was as much a function of the fragmentation of knowledge in modern society as it was a matter of the fragmentation of college curricula. In any case, Newman's universal man was gone forever, and in his place was the specialist, the technologist, the man of singular purpose operating in a society of efficient consumers. The university became, in the last half of the twentieth century, all things to all people, a multi-purpose institution with many missions and many more constituencies.

Characteristics of the Multiversity

The twentieth-century American university has not been without its critics, naturally, and some of the more trenchant have been those who long for the curricular coherence of the past, or for a new coherence that would give a sense of purpose to the present and vision for the future. But in Kerr's view, they have not been visionary enough to satisfy both the demands for coherence on the one hand, and for flexibility in a rapidly changing world on the other. Out of all the conflicting strands of history emerges the unlikely consensus of the modern American 'multiversity':

(1) the English college as the model for undergraduate life;
(2) the German university as the model for graduate research;
(3) the land grant service institution as the model for public involvement in higher education (Kerr, 1982: 18).

The new institution is more than the sum of its constituent parts, yet it is hardly an organic conception.

> In an organism, the parts and the whole are inextricably bound together. Not so the multiversity – many parts can be added and subtracted with little effect on the whole or even little notice taken or any blood spilled. It is more a mechanism – a series of processes producing a series of results – a mechanism held together by administrative rules and powered by money. . . . I have sometimes thought of it as a series of individual faculty entrepreneurs held together by a common grievance over parking. (Kerr, 1982: 20)

Nevertheless, the multiversity remains one of the central institutions in our democratic society, in part because of the national conviction that 'new knowledge is the most important factor in economic and social growth' (Kerr, 1982: viii), but also because 'political and cultural changes in part, originate within it' (Kerr, 1982: 129). It is the diversity of the multiversity that allows it to serve the range of interests that a pluralistic society produces, and consequently it is somewhat of a misnomer to refer to The Multiversity, as if it were an identifiable prototype. The multiversity is best viewed as a continuum along which a diversity of human interests are served (Kerr, 1982: 140), and within which human interests are generated and focused. The multiversity does not merely reflect the society in which it is situated, it helps criticize it and thereby helps form its essential interests. In that respect it plays a dual and conflicting role.

Largely because of this conflicting mission, the multiversity is best governed by a precarious and delicate consensus built painstakingly by adroit academic and administrative leadership. The diverse and conflicting communities that make up the multiversity each have legitimate interests served by conservative faculty who may or may not see the institution in its dynamic complexity. The multiversity can easily become a 'Tower of Babel partially falling apart rather than being held loosely together' (Kerr, 1982: 129). In such circumstances the need for consensus and tolerance becomes abundantly evident. Such a delicate balance is best preserved, Kerr argues, when the 'moderates' are in control, and when the 'extremists' are consequently neutralized. The experiences of the decade between 1963, when *The Uses of the University* was first published, and 1972, when the first postscript was written, showed just how delicate this balance was – even if it did not show how to re-establish it.

Kerr's call for effective and vigorous academic leadership is largely historical; he sees the major periods of academic reform coming during times when there were 'giants' at the helms of America's universities. 'Administrators', rather than 'giants' have ruled during times of relative stability, and they have ruled during the rise of faculty power in the twentieth century. Kerr saw the American educational establishment perched on the verge of cataclysmic change in 1972, change that required for its effective consummation, leadership from the top and from the outside.

The influence of the federal government on higher educational policy has increased inexorably since the end of the Second World War, and particularly since the early 1960s. That influence, Kerr argues, has been both positive and negative, but in the 1970s it became pervasive, invading all institutions of higher learning, not just the selected research universities. Along with the intrusion of the federal government into higher education has come a concomitant demand that the universities serve urban interests as they have rural interests in the past (Kerr, 1982: 132). That pressure involves the universities in the formation of public policy, a role with which they are not always comfortable, and a role which further involves them in questions of access. The distribution of federal largesse brought with it demands for a more equitable distribution of existing educational opportunity, as well as demands for expanded programs within the pale of higher education. The demand for a wider variety of educational programs has put pressure on universities to define their general education offerings more carefully in order to create a more unified intellectual world (Kerr 1982: 119, 132–3).

> The 'improvement of undergraduate instruction' is now a lively and even abrasive subject on many campuses. The need to create 'a more unified intellectual world' that looks at society broadly, rather than through the eyes of the narrow specialist, has now become the insistent demand of students for relevance. The need 'to solve the whole range of governmental problems within the university' is now recognized as the battle over governance. 'How to preserve a margin for excellence' in an increasingly egalitarian society has become a most intense issue. (Kerr, 1982: 132, 133)

These issues have a familiar ring to the student of the history of American higher education.

The student revolts of the 1960s and early 1970s strained the delicate consensus that had made campus life idyllic in the postwar period. But while Kerr recognizes the campus revolts in passing (Kerr, 1982: 132–5), he does not connect them to the larger national traumas of the Vietnam War, the civil rights movement and the women's movement. He does not address the issue of whether the universities ought to be agents of social criticism, and if so, where their moral and intellectual responsibilities might give way to other educational missions. These are difficult questions, and while Kerr's analysis is primarily descriptive, his description is not always neutral. Consider the following passage.

> An almost ideal location for a modern university is to be sandwiched between a middle-class district on its way to

becoming a slum and an ultramodern industrial park – so that the students may live in the one and the faculty consult in the other. M.I.T. finds itself happily ensconced between the decaying sections of Cambridge and Technology Square. (Kerr, 1982: 89)

Slum dwellers may not be quite as sanguine about the presence of the university under such circumstances.

In the face of overwhelming change during the past 20 years, the multiversity has remained remarkably stable. Its stability can be attributed to a number of factors, each of which is an essential characteristic of the American multiversity.

Sources of Stability

The fact that there is no national system of higher education in the United States has meant that institutions have been free to change independently of one another, thereby, retaining both singularity of institutional mission and diversity of student body. The increased demand for higher education during the past 20 years has not had the detrimental effect on the élite research universities that was originally feared. The élite have remained élite; enrollments have been absorbed by community colleges and by expanded capacities of existing colleges which have become more comprehensive (Kerr, 1982: 154). What was feared as a great leveling of academic quality in the face of demands for universal access on the one hand, and the demands of student and faculty activists on the other has not occurred – quality and diversity have been preserved while access has been expanded.

Similarly, the multiversities have a variety of funding sources. This has enabled them to off-set losses in one source with increases in another. It has also required them, in some cases, to seek funding that they might not otherwise seek, thereby eroding some of the control over the long-range planning processes. Nevertheless, the importance of technical expertise and the expanding knowledge base have remained paramount to American society generally, and the academic community has benefited thereby (Kerr, 1982: 155, 156).

Finally, according to Kerr, the faculties have retained substantial control over the multiversities (1982: 156), and they have been a conservative force in matters concerning their own interests. Since they exert substantial influence over matters such as curricular planning and research grants, they have tended to preserve the balance of power in their favor, especially during periods of unrest.

Principles and Assumptions of Kerr's Pragmatism

– The American multiversity is a unique combination of the English college, the German university and the land grant service institution. These functions are contiguous, but not necessarily coherent.

– The multiversity is a mechanism, not an organism; it is 'held together by administrative rules and powered by money' (Kerr, 1982: 20).

– The multiversity is a central institution in our democratic society, primarily because the production of new knowledge is the single most important factor in economic and social growth, but also because political and cultural changes frequently originate within it.

– The multiversity is pluralistic rather than monistic, and serves diverse and often conflicting fields of interests that are balanced through the skillful moderation of administrative leadership.

– The multiversity has intimate connections to the federal government. These connections are both financial and political and concern matters of public policy as well as scientific research and technological innovation.

– The lack of intellectual unity is an acknowledged problem among multiversity communities.

– The absence of a national system of higher education in the United States has facilitated the development of diverse institutions with diverse missions; this has allowed élite institutions to remain élite (Kerr, 1982: 98).

2 The Critical Theory of Jurgen Habermas

The four approaches to general education that have characterized American curricular reform have failed to produce any
lasting models of general education and have left us without any
clearly defined sense of what, if anything, general education
ought to do. Existing general education programs run the gamut
from Essentialist required core programs on the one hand to
Pragmatic distribution requirements on the other. Some are
integrative, some distributive, most combine elements from each
approach in an attempt to satisfy competing interests within the
university or college community. What appears axiomatic to an
Essentialist appears dogmatic and arbitrary to a Pragmatist,
wrong headed to an Idealist and artificial to a Progressive. The
problem is not so much that the four approaches conflict with
one another as that they are infinitely elastic in their application
to specific instances of curricular reform. They evidence the
degree to which the gulf between theory and practice, between
value and fact, between what ought to be and what is possible,
infects and distorts our understanding of the educative process
generally, and the relationship of the university to that process
specifically.

The problem of curricular reform is an instance of the larger
problem of social reform, and like the larger problems of social
reform, will admit of instrumental solutions only in the very
short run, and only within the context of larger value decisions
that may or may not have been consciously made. The problems
of curricular reform must be seen within the larger context of a
society in which instrumental reason has come to dominate all
instantiations of reason, and in which only those problems which
admit of instrumental solutions are recognized as problems.

There is yet another way to an understanding of the problems
of general education, one that takes into account the larger social
context of curricular reform. It is an approach that has its
historical roots in the philosophical thinking of the Frankfurt

School and its followers, most notably Jurgen Habermas (Jay, 1973). The Frankfurt School philosophers were interested in addressing a problem articulated in 1936 by Edmund Husserl in 'Philosophy and the Crisis of European Man' (Husserl, 1965). In that work Husserl argues that science has lost its significance for human life largely because it cannot sustain any connection between the truths of science and the truths of 'practical life'. The science world, while replete with truths of an absolute and eternal character, cannot address man in his human *Lebenswelt* (or life-world) because the perspective of science is objective and value free while the perspective of man is subjective and value laden. The result is an uncertain relationship between human scientific activity and human activity in the pursuit of practical interests. It also results in the devaluation of the human-subjective realm of the *Lebenswelt* because that realm cannot yield nomological knowledge. The epistemological presumption of science is that scientific knowledge is absolutely certain; however, that very certainty precludes science from contributing anything to the valuations and judgments typically made in the uncertain world in which scientists live. As William Leiss, a student of the Frankfurt School, has said, 'With respect to the control of both men and nature we find ourselves in possession of ever more efficient means for the accomplishment of ever more obscure ends' (Leiss, 1972: 132).

The philosophers of the Frankfurt School were openly hostile to the positivistic conception of science that characterized so much of European intellectual life in the years immediately prior to the Second World War. They saw with increasing forboding where the scientistic interpretation of human behavior was leading, and they lamented the derogation of theory to the one-dimensionality of instrumentalism. The positivistic understanding of the social sciences ignored the normative dimensions of human life that were its historic content and substituted for them the illusion of a controlled and managed social order. From the point of view of critical theory a 'value free' science was itself the product of a value: the control and domination of the natural world (Horkheimer, 1972 and 1974). They accept from the phenomenologists the notion that consciousness is intentional and rooted in the immediate world of human desires and expectations, in short, in the world of human values. The central tenet of the Frankfurt School is the notion that there are inescapable epistemological connections between knowledge and human intentions and interests and further, that those connections ought to be thematized and subjected to critical scrutiny. The successes of modern science and especially of modern technology have, in the view of such Frankfurt School thinkers as Horkheimer (1972) and Marcuse (1964), tended to overwhelm human reason with the possibilities of an unparalleled mastery of nature. Such is the power of instrumental reason that it can extinguish critical reason, and thus establish itself as the sole standard for rationality. Any intentions that contravene instrumental reason, or that present possibilities that do not admit of instrumental solution, are outside reason itself and relegated to the realm of 'subjective opinion'. In this atmosphere, it becomes difficult to find a ground from which to launch a critique of the established rationality. The Frankfurt School, and especially Jurgen Habermas, sought such a ground in the connection between knowledge and human interests. Critical theory therefore differs from more traditional instrumental theory in that it is not external to that which it examines in the way that the laws of science are external to objectified nature; rather, critical theory is openly and adamantly interested theory. As Richard Bernstein, philosopher and student of social theory, has said:

> Critical theory aspires to bring the subjects themselves to full self-consciousness of the contradictions implicit in their material existence, to penetrate the ideological mystifications and forms of false consciousness that destroy the meaning of existing social conditions. Critical theorists see the distinction between theory and action which is accepted by advocates of traditional theory, as itself an ideological reflection of a society in which 'theory' only serves to foster the status quo. (Bernstein, 1978: 182)

Habermas addresses the task of grounding a critical theory of society in *Knowledge and Human Interests* (Habermas, 1971). However, his work has recently taken other directions which make him perhaps the most systematic social theorist of his generation. While his work is largely programmatic in nature, it is suggestive of directions for further research. This chapter examines the implications of his theory of human interests and his theory of communication for curricular reform.

THE GROUND FOR A CRITICAL THEORY OF SOCIETY

If it is true, as one Habermas scholar has argued, that the distinction between critical and traditional theory hinges on the explicit recognition of the intimate relationship of knowledge and human interests, then this relationship must be clearly explained (Bernstein, 1978: 180). The relationship in question is the ancient one between what we can know of social life as it exists in the imperfection of the moment, and what we can imagine it to be under more ideal conditions. If traditional theory is concerned with doing things right – that is, with proper technique – then critical-theory is concerned with doing the right things – that is, with an interest in improving the quality of human life. Critical theory has, in short, a fundamental interest in bringing to explicit consciousness the tension between what is and what ought to be. At first it might appear that this is a pseudo-distinction in as much as the quality of modern human life is bound up with the technical prowess of the species, but technical prowess is dependent on value-neutral methodologies whose power resides in disinterested observations and the judicious application of the scientific method. As Habermas explains:

> The progressive 'rationalization' of society is linked to the institutionalization of scientific and technical development. To the extent that technology and science permeate social institutions and thus transform them, old legitimations are destroyed. The secularization and 'disenchantment' of action-orienting worldviews, of cultural tradition as a whole, is the obverse of the growing 'rationality' of social action. (Habermas, 1970: 81)

Much of the argument of *Theory and Practice* (Habermas, 1973) hinges on an appreciation for the changes in social self-understanding from Aristotle to Hobbes, and on the confusion consequent to that changed understanding. Politics, for Aristotle and for the Greeks of the golden age of Athens, was intimately tied to the notion of the *polis*, to the understanding that human *being* was constituted by and in the polis. The most extreme form of punishment in that context was ostracism, which stripped the individual of his humanity by denying him access to politics.

Human being was inconceivable outside the state, and politics was the means through which human being was articulated and realized in the individual through the practice of the good and just life. In that sense politics was an extension of ethics, and subject to the same epistemological limitations: it could not yield nomological and empirically verifiable knowledge.

But for Hobbes, and for the modern understanding of social theory, the situation is quite different. There are natural laws of human behavior that are empirically verifiable, immutable, and technically applicable to all situations and at all times. It is the task of social theory to discover these principles and apply them in technically appropriate fashion to the problems of the modern state. Ethical considerations are appropriate neither to the process of discovery nor to the process of technical application, which is largely a matter of devising human institutions which are consonant with the mechanical laws of nature (Habermas, 1973: 42). Modern social science has this Hobbesian orientation, though in a much more sophisticated form. The confusion between the Greek and modern conceptions of social and political reality define the parameters of the task for critical theory.

> . . . how can the promise of practical politics – namely, of providing practical [that is, ethical] orientation about what is right and just in a given situation – be redeemed without relinquishing, on the other hand, the rigor of scientific knowledge, which modern social philosophy demands in contrast to the practical philosophy of classicism? And on the other, how can the promise of social philosophy to furnish an analysis of the interrelationships of social life, be redeemed without relinquishing the practical orientation of classical politics? (Habermas, 1973: 44)

The problem of finding ground for a critical theory of society must address this conflict between the classical and modern conceptions of social theory. Richard Bernstein has discussed this matter at length in *The Restructuring of Social and Political Theory* (1978) in which he traces the historical development of different conceptions of social theory, including that of the Frankfurt School. His argument, which has been partially recounted above, makes much of the confusion between the practical and the technical in the language of politics. The practical has come to mean the 'expedient' or the technically possible, whereas for Habermas the practical always refers to the processes of interaction within a normative order, and as such is synonymous with the ethical and the political. The confusion is rooted in the disappearance of critical reason and the supremacy of technical reason and the logic of efficiency. We can see the phenomena clearly in the American Progressive Movement of the early twentieth century, of which John Dewey was the primary educational spokesman. Historians disagree as to whether Progressivism as a political program was designed to restructure American society along lines more amenable to an equitable redistribution of economic and political opportunity, or whether it was, rather, a program designed to solidify inequities by scientifically managing some of the more socially explosive crises in the system. The normative assumptions that ground social scientific methodologies have been overshadowed by the successful management of political crises and remain largely unquestioned by the practitioners of social sciences and by those in whose name such crises are managed. Habermas states it plainly:

> Yet even a civilization that has been rendered scientific is not granted dispensation from practical questions: therefore a peculiar danger arises when the process of scientification transgresses the limit of technical questions, without, however, departing from the level of reflection of a rationality confined to the technological horizon. For then no attempt at all is made to attain a rational consensus on the part of citizens concerned with the practical control of their destiny. Its place is taken by the attempt to attain technical control over history by perfecting the administration of society, an attempt that is just as impractical as it is unhistorical. (Habermas, 1973: 255)

To the extent that education is a social science, it is clearly subject to the same caveats as other social sciences in this regard. It is significant that the rapid spread of public school education is contemporary with the Progressive Era and with the scientific administration of virtually all areas of public life. It is also significant that the central tenet of Dewey's philosophy, that personal growth is the goal of education and of all life, is overshadowed by the gains in pedagogical mastery that his insights made possible. The insight that students tend to learn more readily when the content of their learning is directly related to their immediate experience may or may not be used to further the goals of personal growth. The pedagogical techniques that increase learning rates can be ripped from their normative context and used to accomplish 'socially useful' but personally destructive ends. To the extent that Dewey's thought does not recognize this possibility, it must be judged naïve and utopian. To the extent that science is seen as the epistemological standard by which all other forms of knowledge are measured, the practical human interest is either extinguished or deformed.

In *Knowledge and Human Interests* (1971), Habermas seeks to ground the critical theory of society in the human cognitive interests. (For a discussion of how Habermas develops the cognitive interests see the Introduction.) It is important to note that Habermas is not denigrating the knowledge claims of any of the human interests. He is simply arguing that the claims of the empirical-analytical sciences are not the only claims that have legitimacy, and that they ought not to be considered as the models for all other kinds of knowledge. The distinction between what he calls work or 'purposive-rational' action and interaction or 'communicative' action is a critical one. The claims of the empirical-analytical sciences are validated through the scientific method and all of the technical rules that the scientific method implies, while the claims of the historical-hermeneutic sciences are validated through the consensual agreement of intersubjective norms. He says:

> By 'work' or *purposive-rational action* I understand either instrumental action or rational choice or their conjunction. Instrumental action is governed by *technical rules* based on empirical knowledge. . . . By 'interaction', on the other hand, I understand *communicative action*, symbolic interaction. It is governed by binding *consensual norms*, which define reciprocal expectations about behavior and which must be understood and recognized by at least two acting subjects. Social norms are enforced through sanctions. Their meaning is objectified in ordinary language communication. While the validity of technical rules and strategies depends on that of empirically

true or analytically correct propositions, the validity of social
norms is grounded only in the intersubjectivity of the mutual
understanding of intentions and secured by the general recognition of obligations. (Habermas, 1970: 92)

Each of the human interests that Habermas develops in
Knowledge and Human Interests is grounded in one dimension of
human social existence. Wherever we find human beings, we
find them systematically engaging these interests in the reproduction and self-realization of the species. This is perhaps the
most problematic part of his theory, and one that has been
critically received by Hans-George Gadamer and others
(Mendelson, 1979: 44–73). The problem, which is beyond the
scope of this work, centers on the epistemological status of the
human interests, a status that Habermas argues is 'quasi-
transcendental' (Habermas, 1971: 197). In any case, his critical
theory moves from a consideration of the human interests to a
consideration of communicative action, where his philosophical
system has reached its most mature phase. His theory of
communicative action has substantial implications for core
curriculum development and for the development of a critical
theory of education.

THE THEORY OF COMMUNICATIVE ACTION

Habermas has established the need for free and open communication as a necessary condition for the realization of all of the
human interests. The successful description of reality from the
point of view of work and the technical interests that guide it,
requires that a symbolic universe be established in which there
are no systematic constraints on communication. In the academic community these conditions are maintained by the traditions of academic freedom and the intersubjectively established
norms for scientific inquiry and hypothesis verification. The
same may be said for the historical-hermeneutic sciences, where
the verification procedures depend on the ability of the participants to articulate consensual norms (generally through the
interpretation of texts) in a self-critical fashion that frees the
understanding from ideological distortions. The process of free-
ing the understanding from ideological distortions is the purpose

of the emancipatory knowledge-constitutive interest, which is an interest that runs through all knowledge-constitutive interests insofar as their successful realization requires free inquiry. The emancipatory interest can be realized only in a social context in which self-understanding is attained through dialogue with others who are striving for the same kind of understanding. Bernstein suggests that this form of understanding is Socratic.

We can also grasp what Habermas is up to by appealing to a much older model in philosophy, the Socratic model of self-knowledge whereby, through a process of dialogue, the participants achieve self-knowledge and self-reflection which are therapeutic and effect a cognitive, affective, and practical transformation involving a movement toward autonomy (Mundigkeit) and responsibility. (Bernstein, 1978: 199)

As Bernstein further points out, Habermas is drawing an analogy between psychoanalysis and critical theory, suggesting that the same forms of self-analysis are involved in each (Bernstein, 1978: 200–5). Of course, it is not always the case that this kind of dialogue is possible as a matter of historical fact. Distorted communication is far more common than authentic dialogue, and the kinds of institutions that permit authentic dialogue are present only rarely in societies characterized by social relations of domination. But there are sources of historical legitimacy for institutions that sponsor free speech, particularly in the United States and Western Europe. These institutions themselves have, in recent memory, been captured by forces that would extinguish them. Yet a ground from which to break the fetters on free and unconstrained communication was found, and it was found within the nature of communication itself.

It is the central tenet of Habermas' critical theory as well as his theory of communicative competence that within the speech act itself are anticipated the conditions for life free of unnecessary domination. Every speech act presupposes the possibility of authentic communication – even distorted speech acts and strategic communications designed to deceive. In the essay 'What Is Universal Pragmatics', Habermas seeks to show that speech acts as well as language are capable of being 'rationally reconstructed' in formal and universal terms. This means that his investigation will focus on what he calls *communicative compe-*

tence as distinct from the *linguistic competence* that forms the content of the investigations of such linguisticians as Chomsky, Austin and Searle, and others (Habermas, 1979: 1–68). It is important to make the distinction between linguistic and communicative competence clear: Habermas is arguing that speech acts, the most elementary units of communication, have certain universalizable rules, assumptions and objectives that obtain in all communications, regardless of their linguistic form or ideological intent.

> The basic universal-pragmatic intention of speech-act theory is expressed in the fact that it thematizes the elementary units of speech (utterances) in an attitude similar to that in which linguistics does the units of language (sentences). The goal of reconstructive language analysis is an explicit description of the rules that a competent speaker must master in order to form grammatical sentences and to utter them in an acceptable way. . . . A general theory of speech actions would thus describe exactly that fundamental system of rules that adult subjects master to the extent that they can fulfill *the conditions for a happy employment of sentences in utterances*, no matter to which particular language the sentences may belong and in which accidental contexts the utterances may be embedded. (Habermas, 1979: 26)

The competent speaker must produce linguistically comprehensible sentences, but in addition he must also 'fulfill presuppositions of communication' (Habermas, 1979: 27) that cannot be fulfilled by grammatical formulations alone. This communicative competence includes the following abilities:

> The speaker must choose a comprehensible [*verstandlich*] expression so that the speaker and hearer can understand one another. The speaker must have the intention of communicating a true [*wahr*] proposition (or a propositional content, the existential presuppositions of which are satisfied) so that the hearer can share the knowledge of the speaker. The speaker must want to express his intentions truthfully [*wahrhaftig*] so that the hearer can believe the utterance of the speaker (can trust him). Finally, the speaker must choose an utterance that is right [*richtig*] so that the hearer can accept the utterance and

speaker and hearer can agree with one another in the utterance with respect to a recognized normative background. Moreover, communicative action can continue undisturbed only as long as participants suppose that the validity claims they reciprocally raise are justified. (Habermas, 1979: 2–3)

In other words, the statements are made in relation to external reality (that is, the statements claim to be true), internal reality (that is, the speaker claims to be truthful), and normative intersubjective reality (that is, the speaker claims that the statements made are right and appropriate according to the intersubjective norms of the given speech situation). Thomas McCarthy points out the various lines of research these validity claims suggest and indicates the direction in which Habermas' own research is taking him, the establishment of interpersonal relations and the theory of social action (McCarthy, 1978: 281–2).

Every speech act takes place on two levels: the immediate level of interaction within an already achieved consensus (communicative action), in which the communication is comprehensible and assumes truth, truthfulness, and rightness, and on a deeper level on which this background consensus can be thematized and questioned (communicative discourse). In all cases, the implicit assumption in speech acts is that an understanding is possible. For Habermas, this is absolutely fundamental: the act of speech itself presupposes the possibility of understanding and consensus, and is aimed at producing such understanding and consensus. 'What raises us out of nature is the only thing whose nature we can know: *language*. Through its structure, autonomy and responsibility are posited for us. Our first sentence expresses unequivocally the intention of universal and unconstrained consensus' (Habermas, 1971: 314). That this unconstrained consensus is not always present in human interaction, does not obviate the universal certainty of its possibility. All communicative interaction, even 'strategic' interaction that is explicitly designed to deceive and occlude the truth, has as its necessary presumption some manner of understanding – however impoverished it may in fact turn out to be. Much human communication is systematically distorted, either by external constraints or by internal pathologies, but Habermas holds open the possibility that these situations can be rectified through communicative discourse designed to restore the defective background consensus.

The conditions for communication free of systematic and internal distortions are precisely the same conditions for the true and good life.

> However, only in an emancipated society, whose members' autonomy and responsibility had been realized, would communication have developed into the non-authoritarian and universally practiced dialogue from which both our model of reciprocally constituted ego identity and our idea of true consensus are always implicitly derived. To this extent the truth of statements is based on anticipating the realization of the good life. (Habermas, 1971: 314)

Habermas attempts to overcome the separation of the true and the good that is characteristic of our technological and instrumental age, by showing that the conditions for each are identical. One might well speculate about the nature of science and education in closed societies and conclude that in essential respects they can only be retarded by the deformed character of communicative action they sponsor. It is undeniably true, as Thomas McCarthy has pointed out (1978: 288–9), that the four validity claims enumerated above can be viewed as the dimensions in which communicative interaction might break down or become disturbed. In that respect they serve a kind of normative function that keeps communication vital and open to its participants. In the event of a breakdown in communication, the parties to the speech act have certain recourses that depend upon social relations for their vitality.

When the *truth* of a statement is called into question, the speaker may enjoy several strategies of clarification and persuasion within the context of normal interaction. However, as is often the case, what is challenged may be so fundamental as to threaten the communication itself. When that happens, Habermas argues, communication may be broken off or it may be continued at a different and more radical level, the level of *theoretical discourse* in which the rival truth claims are subjected to the force of rational argument. When a *norm* as the basis for communicative action is called into question, the matter can be settled at the level of *practical discourse*. Similarly the other validity claims can be redeemed through communicative discourse of various kinds.

It is crucial for the development of any educational theory, particularly the development of a 'critical' educational theory, that the nature and basis for the background consensus of consensual speech be thematized. Programs of general education have typically attempted to establish this background consensus, although they have not necessarily attempted to provide a critical understanding of it. Programs of liberal education have often attempted a critical analysis of this background consensus at one level or another, but rarely have they established the conditions for free speech, much less for the good life. Core curricula have tended to span the spectrum from those primarily interested in the transmission of inherited cultural values and the inculcation of basic skills, to those that attempt to re-establish the conditions for the just and good life within the college community of scholars. In any case, there is *always* a background consensus against which education takes place, whether or not this consensus is critically embraced. Habermas establishes the general conditions for truth and morality by making a distinction between two forms of communication, communicative action (interaction) and communicative discourse. Communicative action takes place at the level of an assumed background consensus; communicative discourse establishes the background consensus. There are two kinds of communicative discourse: theoretical discourse, which establishes truth claims, and practical discourse which establishes normative claims. One deals with epistemological questions, the other with ethical or moral questions. Before considering the implications of Habermas' theory for a critical theory of general education, it is necessary to flesh out his conceptions of theoretical discourse and practical discourse, and to examine his consensus theory of truth and its implications for the ideal speech act.

Communicative discourse differs from other kinds of discourse in that the participants in communicative discourse agree to put aside all motives other than those concerned with coming to a grounded agreement. The essential assumption operative in discourse is that it is possible to come to agreement, that all other constraints to communication are temporarily set aside in favor of coming to agreement, and that all participants to the discourse genuinely seek to agree on the basis of the better argument, and not merely consequent to the accidental circumstances of their participation. In their fundamental structures, theoretical discourse, which aims at validating truth claims, and practical discourse, which aims at validing problematic norms, are similar. Furthermore, though tied to certain human cognitive interests, the procedures by which truth claims are validated are universal and are grounded in the nature of speech.

Habermas develops a consensus theory of truth for theoretical discourse, in which truth is determined solely by the force of the better argument. He focuses on the propositional content of the utterance and argues that a true statement is one in which intersubjectivity plays the determining role. McCarthy translates the following passage from 'Wahrheitstheorien', (*Wirklichkeit und Reflexion: Festschrift für Walter Schulz*, Pfullingen, 1973):

> I may ascribe a predicate to an object if and only if every other person who *could* enter into a dialogue with me *would* ascribe the same predicate to the same object. In order to distinguish true from false statements, I make reference to the judgment of others – in fact to the judgment of all others with whom I could ever hold a dialogue (among whom I counterfactually include all the dialogue partners I could find if my life history were coextensive with the history of mankind). The condition of the truth of statements is the potential agreement to all others. (McCarthy, 1978: 299)

The propositional content of an assertion by itself is not enough to warrant its truth. One might well make a statement that is true without being able to provide any logical or rational justification for its truth. In such cases, the statement is unwarranted or groundless. Some might argue, for example, that this is the case of the Essentialists who argue for the truth of a given text without being able to warrant that truth on any ground other than a subjective bias or an historical prejudice. It would seem for Habermas that the mere assertion of what seems to be self-evident does not necessarily constitute a warranted truth claim. Only when that claim is placed in the context of the universal rational argument can it be called true. In other words, Habermas claims that we cannot separate the criteria for the truth of a statement from the criteria for the warranted assertability of the statement. One may be certain of something without ever bringing that certainty before the tribunal of collective consciousness; but to claim that a statement is true in the sense of being valid, one must invoke intersubjective corroboration (McCarthy, 1978: 300). The Essentialist must abandon a dogmatic position with regard to the Great Books, and then legitimate those texts in communicative discourse (of both the theoretical and practical type) with others similarly situated.

A rationally motivated consensus can be reached only where there is the possibility of increasingly deeper analysis on increasingly more fundamental levels of reflection. All conceptual frameworks must in principle be open to question when the need arises. This openness is almost certainly counterfactual in most instances, as is amply evidenced in the arguments of Thomas Kuhn (1970), for example. But it must be theoretically possible to examine the conflicting claims of different conceptual frameworks, if the possibility of true consensus is not to be foreclosed. Any agreement based on less than complete examination of the possible conceptual frameworks, is contingent on the particular conceptual framework in which it is stated. Needless to say, this is where the cutting edge of human consciousness resides, and if theoretical frameworks are to be adjusted to meet the anomalies of experiential science, the freedom to question them is essential.

The act of speech itself presupposes the possibility of consensus. Central to Habermas' theory of communicative competence and to his epistemology is the notion of the ideal speech situation, perhaps the clearest articulation of which occurs in McCarthy's introduction to *Legitimation Crisis*.

This absence of constraint, this exclusion of systematically distorted communication . . . can be characterized formally, that is in terms of the pragmatic structure of communication . . . the structure is free from constraint only when for all participants there is a symmetrical distribution of chances to select and employ speech acts, when there is an effective equality of chances to assume dialogue roles. In particular, all participants must have the same chance to initiate and perpetuate discourse, to put forward, call into question, and give reasons for or against statements, explanations, interpretations, and justifications. Furthermore, they must have the same chance to express attitudes, feelings, intentions and the like, and to command, to oppose, to permit, and to forbid, etc. . . . In other words, the conditions of the ideal speech situation must ensure not only unlimited discussion but also discussion which is free from all constraints of domination, whether their source be conscious strategic behavior or communication barriers secured in ideology and neurosis. Thus, the conditions for ideal discourse are connected with conditions for an ideal form of life; they include linguistic conceptualizations of the traditional ideas of freedom and justice. 'Truth', therefore, cannot be analyzed independently of 'freedom' and 'justice'. (Habermas, 1975: xvi–xvii)

These conditions may appear to be utopian, particularly in the context of a thinker as pragmatically oriented as Habermas. His argument is not that these conditions necessarily obtain in every speech situation, though they might appear at any time, but rather that they are the 'unavoidable suppositions' of *discourse* (McCarthy, 1978: 309). Unless we make these suppositions, discourse itself is pointless. When we do make these suppositions, it becomes apparent that the goal of critical theory (namely, the emancipated life) is inherent in Habermas' notion of truth since it is anticipated in every act of communication, whether reflected or not. Critical theory is thus grounded in language, in the very notion of truth itself: the true and the good, instrumental reason and critical reason are reunited.

Habermas' analysis of practical discourse is essentially parallel to his treatment of theoretical discourse, as might be expected from his conclusions regarding the ideal speech situation. His primary concern is to establish that moral questions can be decided discursively and rationally, and that they are not merely the result of subjective bias on the one hand, or instrumental necessity on the other. Again, the most accessible sources for his treatment of practical discourse occur in the essay 'Wahrheitstheorien' (Habermas, 1973b), as translated and interpreted by Thomas McCarthy (McCarthy, 1978). Habermas argues that while there are differences between theoretical and practical discourse, the differences do not exclude from rational discussion matters of practical importance. He argues that there is a rational will which is capable of deciding matters of moral and political importance according to the force of the better (more rational) argument. Furthermore, there is a moral background consensus against which practical speech acts take place, and it is possible to thematize that background consensus in much the same way that it is possible to thematize the background consensus in theoretical discourse, that is, by pushing to increasingly more reflected (or 'radicalized') levels of discourse.

The same presuppositions of freedom from constraint also apply to practical discourse; there must be symmetry and equality and the general freedom from constraints on communication that are necessary for theoretical discourse. But the evidence necessary to support the conflicting claims differs from theoretical discourse.

> We are dealing here with the pragmatic modality of cogency and not with the logical modality of necessity: casuistic evidence, in the form of cogent arguments, provides good reasons or grounds for accepting a proposed explanation or justification. In theoretical discourse the logical gap between evidence and hypothesis is bridged by various canons of induction. The corresponding function in practical discourse is filled by the principle of universalizability: 'only those norms are permitted which can find general recognition in their domain of application. The principle serves to exclude, as not admitting of consensus, all norms whose content and range of validity are particular.' (McCarthy, 1978: 313)

The argument takes an interesting turn at this point, one which makes it possible for Habermas to ground morality in the intersubjective structures of communication. He argues that while practical interests can be subjective and particular, they can also be generalizable through the same processes that all interests can be generalizable. Just as there is a distinction between sense certainty and validity, there is a corresponding distinction between personal desires and generalizable interests. Only the latter become socially binding norms and standards for conduct, because only the latter can be generalized through the principle of universalizability.

The final step in Habermas' argument brings theoretical and practical reason together at the level where what we should want depends on what we can know.

Whereas the critique of knowledge required a thematization of
the interests underlying different forms of inquiry, the critique
of moral-practical consciousness requires asking what we
should want to know, and this depends in turn on what we can
know. Theoretical and practical reason are inextricably
linked; they are moments of a comprehensive rationality
whose coherent development signifies the development of a
rational will. (McCarthy, 1978: 317)

The coherent development of the rational will cannot be
achieved in isolation by a solitary reasoning consciousness since
the very possibility of reason implies intersubjectivity. The
rational will is not 'out there', waiting for the mind of Man to
uncover it, nor is it dwelling within in nascent and contingent
form waiting for the right historical moment. Rather, it is
brought into explicit consciousness through the mutual and
reciprocal processes of communication of which Habermas
speaks. The possibility of the rational will is inherent in human
interests, but becomes rational as it becomes universalized. The
rational will is realized in theoretical and practical discourse, the
aim of which is to come to consensus concerning which human
interests are generalizable. Not all human interests are rational.
Insofar as they are rational, they are affirmable as components of
the rational will. The process through which interests are
universalized is called discursive will formation, and that process
is essential to the human project. For Habermas, the human
species has a moral history just as it has a scientific history.

. . . the moral system can no more simply erase the memory of
a collectively attained state of moral consciousness, once
practical discourses have been permitted, than the scientific
system can retreat behind an attained state of cumulative
knowledge or block theoretical progress once theoretical discourses have been institutionalized. If the moral and scientific
systems follow inner logics, as I am supposing they do, the
evolution of morality, like the evolution of science, is dependent on truth. (Habermas, 1975: 87–8)

Each proposed interest represents a need that competes for
recognition and legitimation within the process of discursive will
formation, though certainly not all needs are generalizable. In

the ideal speech situation, only those interests that are truly generalizable will gain assent, but the ideal speech situation is rare, to say the least. Therefore, since the needs arise in a specific historical situation and can be neither proposed nor affirmed by a disembodied consciousness residing outside of history, the content of any specific generalizable interest will be shaped by the possibilities of that time and place (Habermas, 1975: 95–102). Again the argument seems to run against those who would postulate moral absolutism, since those who are affected by the generalizable interest must perpetually reaffirm it in discursive will formation that approximates the ideal speech situation. This point is particularly important for democracies who may tend to find in their form of political organization the embodiment of some transcendental and immutable principle of truth. Such for Habermas is not the case. He makes a distinction between the legitimating grounds of a political order and the accidental circumstances of any particular political institutions, such that extant institutions are merely the means through which interests are legitimately accommodated (McCarthy, 1978: 331). This statement has far-reaching implications for the development and implementation of curricular reform in institutions of higher education.

In order to better understand the significance of discursive will formation for core curriculum reform, a brief discussion of the central argument of *Legitimation Crisis* (Habermas, 1975) is essential. For it is in *Legitimation Crisis* that Habermas describes the mechanisms through which advanced capitalist societies ground their understanding of themselves.

His argument can be succinctly stated: in modern capitalist democracies there is a radical breach between the actions of the government that are necessary to the preservation of the economic order and the discursively grounded principles upon which the political order is based. To use the language of Habermas, the generalizable interests that may have been rationally grounded in communicative discourse have been suppressed by treating them as particular (Habermas, 1975: 111–17). This amounts to the private appropriation of public wealth by governmental institutions charged with the administration of the 'general welfare'. Their actions would never gain assent in the ideal speech situation –that is, in a communicative environment where the best interests of all concerned could be actively solicited. In this respect *Legitimation Crisis* is a Marxist analysis of contemporary capitalism. Habermas, however, does not find the crisis tendencies of modern capitalism solely, or even primarily, within the economic sphere, as does Marx, but, rather, within the sociocultural sphere where the organizational principles of society do not allow for the rational solution to problems critical to society's continued existence. For purposes of this study, one place such crisis tendencies appear is within the university generally, and within the area of curricular reform particularly, for example, the consensual establishment of a core curriculum is always problematic, and generally treated as a special problem with an instrumental solution. Nowhere is the private appropriation of public resources better served than in the training of the industrial and technical and professional workforce, and in the intimate connections between industry and public education. It is no accident that accrediting institutions often play large roles in the establishment and implementation of new core curricula.

Administrative control of the economic crises that periodically occur in capitalist (and other) economies is limited by the boundary conditions of existing value systems, and when administrative control is lost or threatened from within, there is a 'rationality crisis' (Habermas, 1975: 61–8). Rationality crises threaten the administrative system by questioning its technical mastery. Legitimation crises, on the other hand, threaten the administrative system by calling into question their consonance with existing generalizable interests: it is an *identity crisis*, and as such calls into question the legitimacy of existing modes of social organization. Legitimation crises are 'managed' in the following manner:

> The arrangement of formal democratic institutions and procedures permits administrative decisions to be made largely independently of specific motives of the citizens. This takes place through a legitimation process that elicits generalized motives – that is, diffuse mass loyalty – but avoids participation. This structural alteration of the bourgeois public realm . . . provides for application of institutions and procedures that are democratic in form, while the citizenry, in the midst of an objectively (an sich) political society, enjoy the

status of passive citizens with only the right to withhold acclamation. (Habermas, 1975: 36–7)

This system is the best of both worlds in that it promotes mass loyalty while at the same time ensuring a high degree of administrative independence from those not 'technically qualified' to make decisions. Of course, discursive will formation threatens this system since this system is dependent on a high degree of civil privatism (one might also suggest a high degree of miscommunication). That we no longer 'find ourselves' in the public realm is a truism lamented by no less a conservative philosopher than Allan Bloom (1987), and describes a pervasive attitude toward politics that has predominated at least since the Watergate era. But Habermas points out that the compromise begins to break down as the demands of the administrative system encroach upon the sanctity of the private domain – as government becomes increasingly intrusive in areas previously delimited by the norms of civil privatism. This intrusion weakens social and cultural traditions and calls for a new relation to them.

A rationality deficit in public administration means that the state apparatus cannot, under given boundary conditions, adequately steer the economic system. A legitimation deficit means that it is not possible by administrative means to maintain or establish effective normative structures to the extent required. During the course of capitalist development, the political system shifts its boundaries not only into the economic system but also into the socio-cultural system. While organizational rationality spreads, cultural traditions are undermined and weakened. The residue of the tradition must, however, escape the administrative grasp, for traditions important for legitimation cannot be regenerated administratively. Furthermore, administrative manipulation of cultural matters has the unintended side effect of causing meanings and norms previously fixed by tradition and belonging to the *boundary* conditions of the political system to be publicly thematized. In this way, the scope of discursive will-formation expands – a process that shakes the structures of the depoliticized realm so important for the continued existence of the system. (Habermas, 1975: 47–8)

This legitimation crisis has obvious and extensive implications for education, especially for core curricula. As the private realm undergoes its historical transformations, the educational system is called upon to maintain the stability of the 'depoliticized public realm' by either transmitting existing cultural values or by positing new ones that conform more readily to changing cultural circumstances. But as Habermas points out, 'traditions important for legitimation cannot be regenerated administratively', and in fact they cannot be maintained at all without becoming ideological justifications for the status quo. The task of education is to serve these needs, not necessarily to legitimize them.

> Familial-vocational privatism complements civil privatism. It consists in a family orientation with developed interests in consumption and leisure on the one hand, and in a career orientation suitable to status competition on the other. This privatism thus corresponds to the structures of educational and occupational systems that are regulated by competition through achievement. (Habermas, 1975: 75)

Perhaps more than any other aspect of curricular reform, core curriculum reform addresses the needs of a political system in crisis. It is no accident that the move to abandon core curricula took place during a period when there was an inordinate amount of social dissension. The period from 1968 to 1974 was a legitimation crisis in American democracy, and in American higher education.

PRINCIPLES OF HABERMAS' CRITICAL THEORY

   – The central tenet of the Frankfurt School's critical theory is that there are inescapable epistemological connections between knowledge and human interests, between facts and values, between practices and theories. Those connections ought to be thematized and subjected to critical scrutiny.
   – Critical theory has a fundamental interest in bringing to explicit consciousness the tension between what is and what ought to be. It is fundamentally interested theory, and as such

seeks to restore the normative dimensions of social theory excluded by positivism.

– The empirical-analytical sciences are but one of the ways of connecting human interests to knowledge: they ought not to be considered the model for all other kinds of knowledge.

– The central tenet of Habermas' theory of communicative competence is that the speech act anticipates the conditions of the emancipated life and hence of critical theory.

– Speech acts, the most elementary units of linguistic communication, have universalizable rules, assumptions and objectives that obtain in all communications, regardless of their linguistic form or ideological intent. The explication of these rules, assumptions and objectives is the goal of reconstructive language analysis.

– Among these universalizable rules are the four validity claims: comprehensibility, truth, truthfulness, and appropriateness.

– Every speech act takes place on two levels: the immediate level of interaction within an already achieved consensus (communicative action), and a deeper level on which this background consensus is thematized, questioned, and re-established (communicative discourse).

– The conditions for the ideal speech act are identical with the conditions for the ideal life. They can be formally characterized in terms of the pragmatic structure of communication. Truth cannot be separated from freedom and justice.

– Truth is the product of a consensus achieved under the conditions of free speech. The truth of a statement depends upon the potential agreement of all others.

– There are two kinds of communicative discourse: theoretical discourse, which aims at clarifying truth claims; and practical discourse which aims at clarifying normative claims. The two merge in the formation of the rational will.

– The goal of critical theory, the emancipated life, is inherent in the notion of truth since it is anticipated in every act of communication.

– The process through which interests are universalized is called discursive will formation. The formation of this rational will is an ongoing process.

– In modern capitalist democracies there is a legitimation crisis: a potential contradiction between the actions of the government that are necessary to the preservation of the economic order and the discursively grounded principles upon which that order is based.

  – The legitimation crisis is a crisis in the socio-cultural sphere where education plays an important role.

3 A Critical Theory of General Education

INTRODUCTION

It remains to judge the extent to which the four approaches to general education outlined in Chapter 2 are vitiated or confirmed by the critical theory of Jurgen Habermas, and to develop his theory in terms of a specific critical theory of general education. The special problems of higher education presented by the post-Vietnam era are unique in the history of higher education, insofar as they present problems and possibilities unanticipated by the founders of those four schools, including and maybe even especially Clark Kerr's descriptive analysis of the status quo. The description of the modern multiversity as 'a mechanism held together by administrative rules and powered by money . . . a series of individual faculty entrepreneurs held together by a common grievance over parking' (Kerr, 1982: 20), certainly would be foreign to Cardinal Newman, if not the others. Yet that may well be an accurate description of many of the large research universities today.

If it is an accurate description, and I believe that it is, then the problems of curricular reform are even more urgent than ever. General education reform continues eight years after the publication of Gaff's study (Gaff, 1983), as is evidenced by the unexpected popularity of Allan Bloom's recent treatment of the undergraduate experience, which is the most widely read of the many Essentialist diatribes against the dilution of the liberal learning (Bloom, 1987). His description of the problem is startlingly accurate, even if his analysis of its causes is not. The fact remains that none of the four philosophical approaches to education is adequate to the changed circumstances of this generation of curricular issues, because this generation of curricular issues is framed in the context of one of the most pervasive legitimation crises of American history. In order to 're-legitimate' or authenticate the institutions which comprise the background consensus of American higher education, and of

American life itself, a different approach is clearly needed. The solution to the present legitimation crisis may well be found in the universities, and within the universities, in core curricular programs and all that they inspire.

APPROACHES TO GENERAL EDUCATION: AN ASSESSMENT

The four approaches to general education almost never occur in pure form, and when they do occur in pure form it is almost always under extraordinary conditions – such as Newman founding the Irish university, or Hutchins instituting the Great Books program at the University of Chicago. Yet, in various ways, these assumptions have currency within general education programs: within their structure; within their pedagogy; within the attitudes of the professoriate engaged in them; within the variously structured implementation and oversight committees. Existing programs are justified (legitimated) on the basis of the principles enumerated in Chapter 2. Before discussing how the critical theory of Jurgen Habermas can serve as a critical theory of general education, a comparative evaluation of the salient philosophical orientations of each of the four approaches is appropriate.

The distinction between Idealism, as formulated by Newman, and Essentialism as formulated by Hutchins is often not apparent in conversations involving core curricular and general education programs. It is possible to advocate a Great Books curriculum, and therefore to be considered an Essentialist in the Hutchins mold, and simultaneously postulate an ideal conception of man based on natural law, a conception transparent to human reason (Bloom, 1987). And while it is undeniably true that there are many similarities between Idealism and Essentialism, their differences are also significant.

The Idealist approach to general education is dominated by an epistemological assumption concerning both the source of truth and the conditions for its validation. Its source is transcendental, or at least beyond the clutches of mundane temporality, and the conditions for its validation tend to be based on an ideal coherence. Logical coherence is the final arbiter of the truth of all propositions for the Idealist, and is independent of human judgment insofar as it is a condition for human judgment. The human mind is restless, it probes and pries at nature, and as it does so it discovers truths that yield instrumental value. But the acquisition of those instrumental values never suffices to justify the inquiry: knowledge is not power, or at least its *value* is not instrumental. Since all knowledge is hierarchical, and since the human mind cannot embrace all that can be known in an intuitive leap, the additive process of accumulating knowledge tends to have a certain entropic effect, that is, the combination of the desire for instrumental control and the limited nature of the human mind conspire to fragment knowledge and to give a false sense of security. Such excessive specialization leads to the impoverishment of the understanding and to the perversion of the ends of life, which is philosophical (unified) knowledge.

There is a sense in which the university as an institution requires what no individual can ever do, for while it might be possible to have a unified view of knowledge from an institutional perspective, no single mind can ever encompass that much. The demands of Idealism are unrealistic to the pragmatic sophisticate of the twentieth century. They are especially ideal when housed in the nineteenth-century English college, envisioned as a community of scholars dedicated to the diffusion and dissemination of philosophical and integrated knowledge, a community which is supported by a society of diverse interests all of which place demands on the twentieth-century university to be all things to all people. Nowhere is the contrast between the nineteenth century and the twentieth more stark than in the contrast between Cardinal Newman and Clark Kerr.

Similarly, for the Essentialist, there is an objective standard for truth that is accessible to human reason. The capacity for reasoning can be developed and facilitated through the proper exercise of the understanding. Essentialism is also similar to Idealism insofar as the Essentialist sees the end of man in the full development of intellectual power, though for Hutchins that meant formation of mental habits consonant with the metaphysics of Aristotle and Aquinas. The notion that there is a specific content to the best possible education is peculiar to Essentialism and the Great Books program. The Essentialists also held that the unifying principle of the university is the pursuit of truth for its own sake, but at the same time they thought universities should be judged by the extent to which they engaged in critical thinking about the fundamental issues of their time. Essentialism is a good deal less 'ideal' insofar as it recognizes the inescapable realities of the society in which it is set. Hutchins' curricular reforms were a reaction against both dominant trends in American higher education, trends which tended toward an instrumentally elective curriculum, and against the rising tide of European Fascism that represented the destruction of rational coherence and moral unity. The fundamental and inescapable difference between Idealism and Essentialism is that the Essentialists felt the university served a socially didactic function and the Idealists did not.

Dewey recognized in Newman the 'quest for certainty' which was both the existential fate of man, and also the source of the derogation of the practical in favor of the theoretical. Dewey did not share disdain for the practical that characterized both Idealism and Essentialism, but he did recognize the central problem of modern man as the reconciliation of the instrumental and the moral, the scientific and the ethical. In this he was in good company, as we have seen, but, unlike Habermas, Dewey located the problem in the derogation of the practical (the mundane) by the theoretical (the sacred), and saw the origins of the class society, for example, in the perpetuation of the distinction between doing and thinking. Habermas and the Frankfurt School locate the problem elsewhere, in the extent to which instrumental thinking has overwhelmed *all* thought, especially critical thought. It has done this in the interests of the class in whose name liberal thought was originally sanctified.

Nevertheless, Dewey held that all thinking was interested thinking, and was therefore a reciprocal matter in which the world had its say as well as man. Truth was neither a matter of the correspondence of thoughts with their objects, nor was it a matter of the coherence of thoughts with themselves, but rather a matter of the correspondence of interests with the consequences of behavior. In this theory of interests, Dewey is very close to the later formulations of Habermas.

Dewey is also close to Habermas insofar as he recognizes that communication is the fundamental activity of society, the activity in which society can truly be said to exist. Education plays the central role in this process since it involves the transformation of the quality of experience through the interactions of individuals with their natural and social environments. All of the approaches to general education stress that education plays a central role in our social organization; but Idealism, Essentialism and Progressivism all argue (in slightly different ways) that education is both an end in itself, and the end of man.

As its name suggests, Progressivism was and continues to be a philosophy with an agenda for social change. As an approach to general education, it implies that the content of the curriculum ought to serve the students' *legitimate* interests as members of a democratic society. The connection between the institutions of democracy and the pedagogy of Progressivism are explicit in many places in Dewey's philosophy, but nowhere as explicit as in *Democracy and Education* (1916), where he argues cogently that individuals have no meaning apart from their socially communicated and articulated meaning, and that democracy best promotes the kinds of interactions that are likely to lead to growth. Education which develops the capacities for associated living is by definition moral.

While Idealism and Essentialism are similar in many respects, and while Dewey's philosophy in some ways anticipates Habermas, Pragmatism scarcely qualifies as a philosophy at all. It is much more a description of the status quo in the throes of a legitimation crisis than a philosophy that recommends solutions to critical issues. At least that much may be argued about the Pragmatism of Clark Kerr, who explicitly disavows any prescriptive intent in the 1972 'Postscript' to his book (Kerr, 1982: 147). The university Kerr describes is the university that is now in the process of addressing the problems of curricular reform; the university that is more mechanism than organism, pluralism than monism, and is legitimately connected to the mundane affairs of business and government. While Kerr does not prescribe, his description is clearly selective, and while his attitudes toward that which he describes are ambivalent, they are generally approving.

If one principle of Pragmatism can be culled from the work of people like Kerr (1982) and Riesman (1981) it is that change in complex social institutions like the multiversity, comes slowly and incrementally, and usually as the result of adroit *administrative leadership* rather than as a consequence of any manner of discursively formulated consensus – that is, it is more the result of the instrumental manipulation than critical thought. Wholesale reforms of the kind proposed by Newman, Hutchins, and the Progressives are unlikely to be successful because of the inertia of the institution itself, but also because of its diverse constituencies. Like it or not, the multiversity is here to stay, in all its pluralistic chaos, and it is unlikely that we have the instrumental wherewithal to control it. Kerr seems to be saying that problems that are not amenable to instrumental solutions are not really problems at all, but must be accepted as components of a changed reality. His instrumentalism is of a fundamentally different kind from Dewey's insofar as it is ideologically grounded in the uncritically accepted values of Western technocracy.

The four philosophical approaches to general education fail to establish a ground from which they might be self-reflective. Idealism and Essentialism both legitimate themselves by recourse to transcendental sources of truth and morality, and consequently have a distressing flavor of authoritarianism about them. There is little room in which to reconstitute the sources from which the authority flows, since the authority itself is encased in the ideology of the existing cultural value apparatus. Progressivism grounds itself in Dewey's naturalism, in his theory of instincts, habits and intelligence, which translates itself uncritically into the acquisitive and instrumentally oriented ideology of growth. There is no point in Dewey's thought from which we can determine the difference between growth and decay. In that respect he is naïvely optimistic concerning the fortunes of human development in the twentieth century. Finally, Pragmatism is little help because it fails utterly at being a philosophy at all. It is grounded firmly in the instrumental values of the present, a bewildered drum-major in search of a parade.

A CRITICAL THEORY OF EDUCATION

The Philosophical Grounds

The problem of finding ground for a critical theory of general education is similar to the problem of finding a ground for a critical theory of society: the insights that point the way to the critical theory are embedded in that which is to be criticized. If general education serves as the background consensus for the undergraduate curriculum, the undergraduate curriculum serves, however adequately or inadequately, as the highest expression of the background consensus of the dominant society that supports it. When it fails in that mission, the legitimacy of the university itself is called into question. This is not to say that the background consensus supplied by the undergraduate curriculum is shared by all the diverse interests of the university community itself, but such an understanding is shared to some extent by the interests which both serve and are served by the university. General education, at least potentially, brings within the purview of critical reason the unexamined elements of individual and collective consciousness that constitute, through daily application, the fabric of our cultural lives.

It is no secret that instrumental considerations of curricular planning have the potential to distort the communicative processes necessary for the formulation of a critical theory of general education. There are all kinds of constraints on the kind of unlimited and free communication that Habermas suggests is essential to the ideal speech situation. Such constraints are unavoidable in this imperfect world of enrollment-driven budgets, endowments, and boards of governors. To the extent that these constraints, admittedly external to the educational process itself, are internalized in the educational process, the instrumentally possible has usurped the critically desirable for the student in the classroom – a student who has no particular sensitivity for the finer points of management by objectives.

Much of the literature on general education has suggested that higher education in the United States has lost its way, and that one possible solution to the lack of unity and purpose evidenced in undergraduate curricula is a return to general education programs. Those suggesting such a return are usually of a generation educated in one or another of the four approaches outlined in Chapter 1, and their experiences are so colored. For almost any generation educated in the twentieth century, however, the basic suggestions of John Dewey have a ring of familiarity. The function of the school, he said, was threefold:

(1) to provide a simplified environment for systematic assimilation of a complex civilization;

(2) to provide a 'purified medium of action', that is, to cull from the history of experience and possibility only those ele-

ments consonant with the dominant vision of a better future society; and

(3) to facilitate the democratic principle of social mobility (Dewey, 1916: 24).

One can hear within these functions of the school the human cognitive interests of Jurgen Habermas: the technical interest corresponding to the first function; the practical interest corresponding to the second function; and the emancipatory interest corresponding to the third function. Dewey did not develop a philosophy based on these functions because the problems that focused Habermas did not yet speak to the pre-Fascist world in which Dewey was writing. Now that the world has experienced Fascism (perhaps the most pathological disturbance of communicative processes in the history of human speech), the philosophy of Habermas has a compelling urgency.

It has been an assumption of this study from the outset that education serves an emancipatory function, at least in the historical sense of 'liberal education', but also in the more specifically political sense of a critique of ideology. If education maintains the tension between what is and what ought to be in the broad sense of Dewey's three functions, general education must be especially attentive to this possibility in regard to the third function – to facilitate the democratic principle of social mobility. The difference between Dewey and Habermas in this respect is that, while Dewey assumes the legitimacy of the principle of social mobility, Habermas grounds that principle itself in the fundamental nature of the only thing whose nature we can really know – language.

Similarly, the critical theory of general education is grounded in the communicative process itself. By applying Habermas' theory of communicative competence to the communicative processes that articulate general education, it is possible to gain a philosophical basis beyond the immediately ideological from which such programs can be judged. There are three levels of application for Habermas' theory: the initial level of conceptualization and planning, during which the particular general education program is articulated; the implementation and maintenance level through which the general education plan is actuated and adapted to the unforeseen circumstances of academic life; and the pedagogical level in which the program is delivered to the student in the classroom. The theory of communicative competence applies to all three levels of application, and the extent to which communication at all three levels meet the criteria of Habermas' theory measures the extent to which the programs thus conceived are legitimate.

The profoundly critical nature of Habermas' theory of communicative competence can perhaps best be seen by fleshing out the analogy between psychoanalysis and critique. In *Knowledge and Human Interests* (1971: 214–45), Habermas draws a very selective analogy between critical theory and psychoanalysis in which he seeks to show that the goal of each is self-understanding through self-reflection. The psychoanalyst seeks not only to penetrate the patient's self-understanding, but to move the patient to recollect and reconstruct his own self-understanding. This the analyst cannot do for the patient any more than the patient can do it for himself by attending lectures and reading books about psychoanalysis. It is not enough to describe the distorted self-understanding, the patient must internalize the insights by instituting and perpetuating a process of *self-reflection*. The patient is 'cured' to the extent that he maintains the habits of such a self-reflection and carries them on through his future experiences. The purpose of this analogy is to show how a critique of ideology depends upon such a self-reflective process. The same analogy is applicable to general education at all three levels of application.

During times of legitimation crisis the curriculum is understood in the context of distorted communication. The ground from which it can be reformed cannot be found externally to those who constitute and perpetuate it. It can only be found through a self-reflective process in which the 'patient' seeks to understand the nature of the distortions and to acquire the wherewithal to re-establish connections to the sources of curricular authority. Where is the analyst in this situation? Who has the undistorted and clear vision required to lead the way out of the dark wood of error? For Habermas the critical theorist plays an analogous role to the psychoanalyst and, as we have seen, finds visual acuity in the theory of communicative competence.

The Articulation and Planning Phase

Free and open communication is a necessary condition for the realization of all the human interests. Within the undergraduate curriculum, the human interests are represented in systematic form, and such free and open communication as Habermas describes is at a premium. This is partly due to the nature of the disciplines themselves; many courses taught in the under-graduate curriculum do not lend themselves to communicative interaction at all, much less free and open communicative interaction. But it is also due to the structure of the institution within which power relationships distort communication as readily as any other workplace in a complex society (one hears the words of Clark Kerr describing the university being held together by a common grievance over parking). Nevertheless, in every communication, distorted or not, there is a supposition that agreement is possible, and that the relations of authentic communication, though usually counterfactual, are within the grasp of participants to the speech act. When this supposition is not present, communication becomes strategic, that is, people dissemble and manipulate the communicative process, or com-munication breaks off. Both are real possibilities within the curriculum planning process.

The surprising popularity of Bloom's recent book on the undergraduate curriculum underlines the willingness of the general populace to consider the seriousness of the current legitimation crisis in higher education. In a chapter entitled 'The Student and the University' Bloom states the problem succinctly:

> . . . the crisis of liberal education is a reflection of a crisis at the peaks of learning, an incoherence and incompatibility among the first principles with which we interpret the world, an intellectual crisis of the greatest magnitude, which consti-tutes the crisis of our civilization. But perhaps it would be true to say that the crisis consists not so much in this incoherence but in our incapacity to discuss or even recognize it. (Bloom, 1987: 346)

This inability to discuss or recognize curricular incoherence is a problem Habermas' theory of communicative competence is peculiarly suited to address. When the existence of a communi-cation crisis of this magnitude becomes part of the popular public consciousness, the time has come to address it systema-tically.

The question is not how to structure the undergraduate curriculum so much as how to structure the communicative context in which the undergraduate curriculum is to be addressed. If the problem is a matter of communicative dissonance, that is, if the problem stems from pathologically disturbed communication processes, then the critical theory of general education must address those processes in much the same manner as psychoanalysis addresses the disturbed personality. The analogy is selective, of course, and is only appropriate insofar as it indicates the degree to which the recovery of the patient is dependent upon increasingly reflective self-understandings that continue beyond the immediate solutions proposed. In that respect, the initiation of the process of curricular reform must be carefully conceived, or the process will reproduce the dissonances it was designed to overcome.

The impulse to redesign existing core curricula or to initiate a core program where none previously existed arises out of an assumption that there is some common ground out of which the educational experience ought to grow. The process of articulating and planning a general education program is the single most important problem facing institutions of higher education today, because it amounts to an articulation of the purposes of the university and the purposes of the society of which it is a most essential expression. If the university itself cannot find a background consensus from which to address the technical, practical and critical interests of the species, then communication itself is endangered, and so is democratic life as we know it.

Habermas has argued that every speech act takes place on two levels: on the immediate level of interaction within an already achieved consensus (communicative action), and on a deeper level in which this achieved consensus can be thematized and questioned (communicative discourse). The impulse to reform general education, an impulse that often reinstitutes programs abolished in the 1960s, reflects the breakdown of the background consensus which not only integrates the undergraduate curriculum, but which makes speech itself possible. The early stages of the articulation and planning process are typically characterized by *misunderstandings*, accusations, recriminations, and the entire repertoire of strategic behaviors. Faculty members talk past one another, struggle to find something upon which they can agree, so that they can unify themselves and protect what they perceive to be threats to their autonomy – an autonomy characterized by the dictates of instrumental reason and the specialized interests of the society they are empowered to serve. Administrators conspire to find ways to budget for new programs that will leave existing programs intact and not require increased funding. Meetings designed to reach agreement are often frustrating and confusing displays of administrative and faculty impotence; neither side is able to communicate effectively with the other because there is a fundamental lack of trust.

These communicative distortions are addressed by a serious consideration of Habermas' communicative theory. Communicative competence requires that statements made by both sides to the dispute are comprehensible, true, truthful, and appropriate. All four of these conditions must be met before there can be authentic communication. The speech-act assumes that it is possible to meet these requirements in general, even though such requirements may not be met in any particular speech-act, and when distortions occur, they can be rectified in communicative discourse. The initial stages of the process of curricular reform are particularly susceptible to distorted communication because the participants in the reform process have different agendas proposed by different constituencies, and each recognizes legitimacy only within a very narrow sphere of power and interest.

The renewed interest in general education is a *reform movement*, even when it is aimed at the creation of a new constellation of educational experiences. Some general education program is always operative as a background consensus to any communication system. Where there is no self-reflective program, the assumptions of the background consensus are uncritically accepted as legitimate. This is the dogma of instrumental reason, of Pragmatism, in the contemporary multiversity. The problems of general education then become largely administrative matters – the allocation of teaching assignments within the various academic departments, the allocation of distribution requirements among the various administrative units of the college, the application of transfer credits from other institutions, and other similar instrumental concerns. These are certainly important questions that need to be addressed reflectively, but they are also questions that assume affirmative answers to other more fundamental questions that may not have been asked.

Habermas' theory of communicative competence suggests ways in which the more fundamental questions might be set. When it is no longer obvious what an undergraduate ought to know and how he ought to know it, the background consensus of the academic community has been called into question, that is, there is no longer any consensus about what the operative background to speech-acts (to education) means. A consensus can be reached only where there is the possibility of radicalizing the discussion, namely, of pushing it to increasingly more reflective levels of understanding. This means, as Habermas has argued, that *all conceptual frameworks* must in principle be open to question, reflection and discussion. The possibility of true consensus is not foreclosed as long as the question has been announced.

The announcement can come from any one of several sources – academic, administrative, political and even from the students themselves. It often comes from all of these directions simultaneously in the form of a generalized dissatisfaction with the 'quality' of undergraduate education. The way the question is framed is crucially important for future discussions, and is more than a mere practical matter. Special care must be taken to ensure that the problem is understood as a critical issue in curricular planning, and not a problem susceptible to merely administrative or instrumental solution. The problem-posing stage of curricular planning is an area that begs further research.

Once the problem has been articulated as a matter for communicative discourse, in which all parties to the discourse agree to suspend all motivations other than those that will lead to consensus, and to set aside all constraints to communication in favor of coming to agreement on the basis of the force of the better argument, the serious discussion of what general education ought to be can begin. We can judge this stage of the process by the extent to which it meets these conditions, by the extent to which it stimulates the conditions for free and open discourse on the matter of what the undergraduate ought to know. Again, this assumes that there is something that the undergraduate ought to know, and that we can agree on what it is through the process of rational discourse.

In this regard, Habermas' consensus theory of truth indicates that the standard for judging one proposal better than another is a matter of intersubjective agreement, but intersubjective with a difference: the content of the specific proposal by itself is not enough to warrant its truth – merely uttering apparently self-evident propositions does not pass for truth in this context. It is precisely because these self-evident truths have been uncritically accepted that the problem of curricular reform arose in the first place. It is not enough, for example, to assert as self-evidently true that all undergraduates ought to read *King Lear*, or The *Odyssey*, or that they all ought to have a course in the History of Civilization, or Calculus. It may be that all would agree to these propositions, but curricular reform is a matter of re-establishing for ourselves, the participants in the process of reform, the reasons for inclusion of these great texts and essential experiences. The mere assertion of their greatness does not warrant their truth. The reason *Odyssey* is a great text, for example, is because what Homer says about the human condition is fundamentally *true*, and that truth must be rediscovered in the process of curricular reform. In other words, the process of curricular reform needs to address matters of specific content and their conceptual frameworks in a radically discursive fashion.

The process of rediscovering the truth of great texts, while but one of many problems that need to be addressed by any articulation and planning group, may be seen as a metaphor for the process of curricular reform. (It may not be too outlandish to propose that there is a metaphorical connection between the process of curricular reform and The *Odyssey* itself, insofar as each is a process of 'coming home' that is fraught with danger and confusion, and which depends upon a listening posture toward the world.) Whatever mechanism is devised to articulate the general education program it ought to be judged by the standards articulated by Habermas' ideal speech situation, which have already been articulated in Chapter 3. In order to fulfill the symmetry requirement, the articulation mechanism (committee) must be structured so as to ensure that each member has an equal chance to initiate and perpetuate *discourse*, that is, to force the dialogue to ever more reflected levels whenever the need arises. This means that there must be a possibility for unlimited discussion of each proposal made, and for discussion at whatever levels will result in a resolution through the force of the better argument. In some cases this may mean that individual participants to the process will need to be educated to the special problems of discursive will formation – the process of curricular reform is itself an educational process.

The dictates of the ideal speech situation also imply that each participant will have the same opportunities to express opinions, to vent frustrations, to command, forbid, oppose, and so on. The articulating group (committee) must be structured so that the external power relations brought to the discussion from the university community do not interfere with the process of free speech. This may be the most difficult of all the requirements, and may be the point at which the entire project fails. Unless the participants to the speech-act agree to suspend their special power relationships in the process of reaching consensus on the fundamental nature of truth, they cannot expect to have a general education program that does anything more than perpetuate the distortions of the current educational experience. To this extent, it may be unwise to appoint high-ranking administrative officials to chair the committee, that is, it may be unwise to transport into the process of curricular reform the very structures that make the reform necessary. The tendency is to adopt a committee structure that parallels the structure of the university which is theoretically hierarchical (and which parallels the administrative organization of the industrial apparatus it supports), but such a tendency should be resisted unless it can meet these stringent requirements of symmetry and free speech.

In the final analysis, as Habermas argues, the conditions for ideal discourse are identical with the conditions for the ideal form of life, and the conditions for ideal curricular reform are identical with the conditions for effective teaching and learning within the context of general education, 'they include linguistic conceptualizations of traditional ideas of freedom and justice. "Truth," therefore, cannot be analyzed independently of "freedom" and "justice"' (Habermas, 1975: xvii). In other words, the articulation committee must create among themselves the very environment they hope to extend to the rest of the university – if they cannot do that, the reform project will certainly fail. It may be that there are those on this committee who want it to fail, and if that is the case, they must be converted or neutralized by the force of rational consensus.

The conditions for the ideal speech-act are the 'unavoidable suppositions' of *discourse* (McCarthy, 1978: 309). They may not be explicit at every stage of the articulation process, but they are implicit at every stage because if they were not, communication would break off. When the assumptions are made explicit by employing them as standards by which to judge the authenticity of the discourse, the goal of critical theory and the goal of a critical theory of education merge: the emancipated life is the reflected life. The goal of general education is to explore the conditions of truth, freedom and justice – the background consensus for the 'good life'.

Communicative discourse is either theoretical or practical, either oriented toward matters of truth or matters of morality. The conditions for each are the same, and the implications for each in the formulation of a general education program are the same. The same presuppositions of free speech apply to practical discourse: there must be symmetry and equality and general freedom from constraints on communication. But when communicative discourse is practical, the principle of universalizability comes into play. Since matters of practical interest are not reducible to the canons of logic, they must be submitted to the force of intersubjective validation. Not all practical interests are generalizable; only those are generalizable which can stand the scrutiny of discursive will formation. Since the human species has a moral history just as it has a scientific history, the interests that arise in any particular historical situation can be generalized only by the possibilities of that time and place. This means that the process of curriculum planning, especially general education curriculum planning, is an ongoing process that can never rest secure in any given set of courses or texts. Moral absolutism is neither a theoretical nor a practical possibility since those who are affected by a general education program, which recommends a set of generalizable interests both theoretical and practical, must perpetually reaffirm it in discursive will formation that approximates the ideal situation.

Each institution has particular needs and resource limitations that must be recognized in the planning stages. Such limitations as library resources, student–faculty ratios, institutional type and student–body composition, all contribute to the horizon of limitations and possibilities. The articulation phase amounts to a reconsideration of the role of the institution in relation to the constituencies that comprise it and support it. Insofar as the process recognizes and maintains the ideal speech situation in its deliberations, the conflicting interests of each constituency may be rationalized and universalized in a general education program that is grounded in the reconciliation of instrumental and critical reason.

The Implementation and Maintenance Phase

In the case of a new program, there must be a mechanism for implementation. In the case of a reformed program, there must be a mechanism that ensures that the reforms are carried out under conditions that will promote free and open communication according to the principles of the rationally formed consensus. This stage of general education reform presupposes that the prior stage was carried out properly according to the principles of communicative competence. If that stage was not so articulated, it is doubtful that the implementation phase can correct it. But if the articulation phase was properly executed, the implementation phase continues its work and acts as the central academic institution of the university by continuing to execute the critical theory of general education. For this reason it is critically important that there be continuity between the two stages of the process.

The critical functions of this stage of curricular reform are two:

(1) to oversee the implementation of the articulated general education program; and

(2) to serve as liaison between the faculty in the general education classroom and the rest of the institution.

There are other administrative and personnel functions that are adjunctive to these two major functions, but they are beyond the scope of this philosophical study. It is inconceivable, however, that any administrative function would fall outside the dictates of the theory of communicative competence.

The implementation phase is, from the point of view of critical theory, the continuation of the process of discursive will formation, and the analogy between psychotherapy and critical theory is nowhere more appropriate than here. The implementation process is the process of continued self-reflection by which the university heals itself. It is not enough that the disorder be diagnosed, the components of its recovery must be lived out in the process of critical reflection. Specific questions concerning such issues as faculty recruitment, course selection and review, evaluation of faculty performances and course content, are all matters that enliven the process of creating a university, and ought to be central to the life of the institution. That such functions have been viewed as administrative chores is indicative of the extent to which instrumental reason has overwhelmed critical reason. Matters of faculty recruitment and selection for the general education program, for example, are not matters for administrative decision, but rather, go to the heart of the issue of educational practice.

The Delivery Phase

The delivery phase focuses on the most visible aspect of general education: the classroom experience. However, to begin the process of general education reform by looking at the classroom is to misunderstand the dynamics of the educative process. The students in general education programs are not being asked to form the background consensus against which the university understands itself, for that consensus has already been formed without them. They are coming into a language universe that existed before them and will no doubt exist after they are gone regardless of whether, as individuals, they embrace it or not. But if general education programs are to be understood as authentic educational experiences, experiences in which there is a mutual transformation of consciousness on both sides of the communicative exchange, the ideal speech situation must also be re-created in the classroom – at least to the extent that the force of the better argument can prevail.

There are obvious inequalities in the relations between students and teachers that do not exist in the relations among faculty. But to the extent that education is communication, there is nevertheless the presumption that agreement is possible, that, if the student could equalize himself in all other aspects, he would also assent to the propositions of the general education program. And, like the patient in therapy, the student must assume an active role in the process. To that extent at least, the requirements of the ideal speech situation (for free and unlimited discussion) obtain in the classroom as well. Those courses that are not amenable to *discourse*, are not properly general education courses, for example, basic skills courses are not general education courses, and neither are introductory surveys intended to provide instrumental skills for the beginning major. There may be all kinds of reasons for including these courses in a general education program, but none of them would survive the test of generalizability, which is to say they are reflections of particular interests, however cherished.

It is not necessary to examine the content of any particular general education program to articulate the standards by which that content might be critically assessed. The primary criterion of assessment for courses that seek to communicate, investigate and articulate the background consensus of the university is that they be taught in such a way that they lead to the realization of the conditions for the just and good life. They must actively involve the student in the pursuit of truth, understood as consensus. The primary distinction here is between training and education, between what Paulo Freire calls the 'banking concept of education' and 'problem-posing education' (Freire, 1984: 57–74). The teacher is not the narrating subject who 'possesses' what the listening objects must dutifully accept, attractive as this fiction might seem to certain Essentialist commentators on the subject (Bloom, 1987). The students are not mere passive receptacles into which deposits are made for later withdrawals. Nor are their minds some sort of muscle that needs discipline and training. The students have inherent dignity, they have the same rights to the free speech-act as any other participant in communicative discourse, and they frequently make important contributions to the process of discursive will formation. Since each generation must reaffirm the connections to the true and the just, and since each generation of college students seems to be more heterogeneous than the last, general education must be seen as a valuable contribution to this process.

The salvation of the university lies in the communicative interaction among students and the faculty of general education courses. The university can remain a vital and critical part of society only if free and open communications are encouraged and facilitated. If general education is viewed as the process of inculcating future generations with the values, beliefs, and practices of the dominant society – even if that society is formally democratic – the recipients of such an education will be unable to generate the new communicative relations necessary to sustain democracy, and legitimation crises will be unavoidable. If values are presented as received truths, rather than as the consequences of arduous critical thinking by particular people struggling with timeless questions of human existence, those upon whom such truths are bestowed certainly will become 'value illiterate'; they will be unable to 'read' the signs and symbols of their times.

Glossary of Philosophical Terms

(1) Communicative action: speech as well as other non-verbal forms of communication that require a background consensus of meaning that is either accepted or taken for granted, and that results in action.

(2) Communicative discourse: speech and non-verbal forms of communication that occur when the background consensus is disturbed or no longer taken for granted. Communicative discourse tests competing truth claims with the force of the better argument, and therefore produces arguments but not action.

(3) Consciousness, reflective: the operative mode of intentional consciousness that takes itself as the object of its intention.

(4) Consciousness, unreflected: the operative mode of intentional consciousness that has objects of intention other than itself.

(5) Critical reason: reason that serves the interests of individual and species emancipation from the economic, political, and cultural strictures of the status quo.

(6) Facticity: the obstacles to human freedom such as place, past, surroundings, fellow human beings, and death – those dimensions of human existence over which the power to affirm or negate has no effect (Sartre, 1956).

(7) Human cognitive interests: the knowledge-constitutive interests that define both the objects and categories of knowledge and the procedures for discovering and validating truth claims.

(8) Human interests: Habermas defines human interests as: 'The basic orientations rooted in specific fundamental conditions of the possible reproduction and self-constitution of the human species, namely work and interaction' (1971: p. 196). Such human interests do not aim at the satisfaction of empirical needs *per se*, but at the solution of systems problems in general.

(9) Instrumental reason: reason that organizes efficient means

appropriate to the effective control and manipulation of reality.

(10) Nomological knowledge: knowledge which relates to or expresses physical laws or rules of logic.

(11) Technological reason: a special application of instrumental reason that orders and consolidates productive techniques for the purpose of manipulating and controlling nature, including human nature.

Bibliography

Adler, Mortimer, *The Paideia Proposal: An Educational Manifesto* (New York: Macmillan, 1982).

Bernstein, Richard J., *The Restructuring of Social and Political Theory* (University of Pennsylvania Press, 1978).

Bloom, Allan, *The Closing of the American Mind: How Higher Education Has Failed Democracy and Impoverished the Souls of Today's Students* (New York: Simon & Schuster, 1987).

Boyer, Ernest L., *High School: A Report on Secondary Education in America* (New York: Harper & Row, 1983).

Boyer, Ernest L. and Hechinger, Fred M., *Higher Learning in the Nation's Service* (Washington, DC: Carnegie Foundations for the Advancement of Teaching, 1981).

Boyer, Ernest L. and Kaplan, Martin, *Educating for Survival* (New Rochelle, NY: Change Magazine Press, 1977).

Boyer, Ernest L. and Levine, Art, *A Quest for Common Learning* (Washington, DC: Carnegie Foundations for the Advancement of Teaching, 1981).

Culler, Dwight A., *The Imperial Intellect: A Study of Cardinal Newman's Educational Ideal* (New Haven and London: Yale University Press, 1955).

Dewey, John, *Democracy and Education* (New York: Macmillan, 1916).

Dewey, John, *Human Nature and Conduct* (New York: Henry Holt, 1922).

Dewey, John, *Experience and Nature* (La Salle, Illinois: Open Court Publishing Company, 1959, originally published in 1925).

Dewey, John, *The Quest for Certainty: A Study of the Relation of Knowledge and Action* (New York: G.P. Putnam's Sons, 1960, originally published in 1929).

Dewey, John, *How Do We Think: A Restatement of the Relation of Reflective Thinking to the Educative Process* (Boston: D.C. Heath, 1933).

Freire, Paulo, *Pedagogy of the Oppressed*, trans. by Myra Bergman Ramos (New York: Continuum, 1984).

Gaff, Jerry, *General Education Today: A Critical Analysis of Controversies, Practices, and Reforms* (San Francisco: Jossey-Bass, 1983).

Gideonse, Harry D., *The Higher Learning in a Democracy: A Reply to President Hutchins' Critique of the American University* (New York: Farrar & Rinehart, 1937).

Goodlad, John I., *A Place Called School: Prospects for the Future* (New York: McGraw-Hill, 1984).

Gros Louis, R. P., 'General Education: Rethinking the Assumptions' (Change, September 1981).

Habermas, Jurgen, *Toward A Rational Society: Student Protest, Science and Politics* trans. by Jeremy J. Shapiro (Boston: Beacon Press, 1970).

Habermas, Jurgen, *Knowledge and Human Interests* trans. by Jeremy Shapiro (Boston: Beacon Press, 1971).

Habermas, Jurgen, *Theory and Practice* trans. by John Viertel (Boston: Beacon Press, 1973).

119

Habermas, Jurgen, 'Wahrheitstheorien', *Wirklichkeit und Reflexion. Festschrift für W. Schulz* (ed. H. Fahrenbach), (Frankfurt/Main: Pfullingen, 1973b).

Habermas, Jurgen, *Legitimation Crisis* trans. by Thomas McCarthy (Boston: Beacon Press, 1975).

Habermas, Jurgen, *Communication and the Evolution of Society* trans. by Thomas McCarthy (Boston: Beacon Press, 1979).

Habermas, Jurgen, *Theory of Communicative Action* Vol. I trans. by Thomas McCarthy (Boston: Beacon Press, 1984).

Hahn, Lewis E., 'Dewey's Philosophy and Philosophic Method', in *Guide to the Works of John Dewey* (ed. Jo Ann Boydston), (Carbondale, Illinois: Southern Illinois University Press, 1970).

Hall, James W. and Kevles, Barbara L., *In Opposition to Core Curriculum: Alternative Models for Undergraduate Education* (Westpoint, Conn.: Greenwood Press, 1982).

Hegel, G.W.F., *The Philosophy of History* trans. by J. Sibree (New York: Dover, 1956).

Hegel, G.W.F., *The Phenomenology of Mind* trans. by J.B. Bailee (London: Allen & Unwin, 1966).

Hofstadter, Richard, and Smith, Wilson (eds), *American Higher Education: A Documentary History* Vol. I (Chicago: University of Chicago Press, 1961).

Horkheimer, Max, *Critical Theory* trans. by Matthew J. O'Connell et al. (New York: Seabury Press, 1972).

Horkheimer, Max, *Critique of Instrumental Reason* trans. by Matthew J. O'Connell et al. (New York: Seabury Press, 1974).

Husserl, Edmund, *Phenomenology and the Crisis of Philosophy* trans. by Quentin Lauer (New York: Harper & Row, 1965).

Hutchins, Robert Maynard, *The Higher Learning in America* (New Haven: Yale University Press, 1936).

Hutchins, Robert Maynard, *Education for Freedom* (Baton Rouge, La: Louisiana State University Press, 1947).

Hutchins, Robert Maynard, *The Conflict in Education* (New York: Harper & Brothers, 1953).

Jay, Martin, *The Dialectical Imagination: A History of the Frankfurt School and the Institute of Social Research 1923–1950* (Boston: Little, Brown, 1973).

Kerr, Clark, *The Uses of the University* 3rd edn (Cambridge, Mass.: Harvard University Press, 1982).

Kuhn, Thomas, *The Structure of Scientific Revolution* (Chicago: University of Chicago Press, 1970).

Leiss, William, *The Domination of Nature* (Boston: Beacon Press, 1972).

Marcuse, Herbert, *One DimensionalMan* (Boston: Beacon Press, 1964).

McCarthy, Thomas, *The Critical Theory of Jurgen Habermas* (Cambridge, Mass. and London: M.I.T. Press, 1978).

Mendelson, Jack, 'The Habermas-Gadamer Debate', (New German Critique, 18, 1979).

Merleau-Ponty, Maurice, *The Phenomenology of Perception* trans. by Colin Smith (London: Routledge & Kegan Paul, 1962).

Newman, John Henry, *The Idea of University* (New York: Longman's Green, 1947, originally published in 1873).

Riesman, David, *On Higher Education: The Academic Enterprize in an Era of Rising Student Consumerism* (San Francisco: Jossey-Bass, 1981).

Rudolph, Federick, *Curriculum: A History of the American Undergraduate Course of Study Since 1636* (San Francisco: Jossey-Bass, 1977).

Sartre, Jean-Paul, *Being and Nothingness: An Essay on Phenomenological Ontology* trans. by Hazel Barnes (New York: Philosophical Library, 1956).

Soltis, Jonas, 'On the Nature of Educational Research', (Educational Researcher, December 1984).

Whitehead, Alfred North, *The Aims of Education* (New York: Macmillan, 1929).

Index